T3-BNT-598

Clear and Simple Guide to Resume Writing

Marian Faux

MONARCH
PRESS
New York

Abridged and updated edition of The Complete Resume Guide

Copyright © 1980 by Marian G. Faux
All rights reserved
including the right of reproduction
in whole or in part in any form.
Published by Monarch Press
A Simon & Schuster Division of
Gulf & Western Corporation
Simon & Schuster Building
1230 Avenue of the Americas
New York, New York 10020

MONARCH PRESS and colophon are trademarks
of Simon & Schuster, registered in the
U.S. Patent and Trademark Office.

Designed by Irving Perkins
Manufactured in the United States of America
10 9 8 7 6 5 4

Library of Congress Catalog Card Number: 81-84684

ISBN: 0-671-44678-9

650.14
F271
c.3

Contents

Introduction

A resume is your chief job-hunting tool. It serves to introduce you to prospective employers and tells why you would be a valued employee. A well-prepared resume shows off your organizational and writing skills. Perhaps most important, though, a resume, along with the cover letter that accompanies it, is your way of asking for an interview.

Almost everyone needs a resume. Even if you have never written one before, or you think that one is not needed for the kind of jobs you are seeking, you cannot go wrong writing a resume. A resume shows that you are a serious job hunter and that you would be an equally serious employee. It shows that you know how to climb the ladder toward business success. And a resume is one way to stay a step ahead of the competition.

In your search for a job, you will do few things more important than preparing a resume. It is worth all the time and effort that it demands. There should be nothing gimmicky about your resume, though; it is really a simple, straightforward business report. You need to know what to include in your resume, as well as what to omit; how to organize it in an acceptable format; and how to make copies. You also need to know how to circulate your resume to the right people and how to write that all-important cover letter. All this—and everything else you need to know to write a resume that will help you get the right job—are included in this *Clear and Simple Guide to Resume Writing*.

THE CONTENT OF A RESUME

Once you have determined what kind of job you want, you can begin to think about what goes into your resume. Resumes are highly personal and individual. They vary with the kind of job you are seeking. If you are an engineer or a home economist, or have had several years of work experience, you may find yourself with several possible directions to go in search of a job. These directions may require preparing not one but several resumes, each geared to a specific category of job. Then, too, you may have an opportunity to go for a very special kind of job, and you will want to write a resume especially for that. The more skilled you are, the greater the chance that you will require two or more resumes to meet your job-hunting needs. Fortunately, once a basic resume has been prepared, as well as a file of information on yourself that you can constantly update, spin-off resumes are fairly simple to prepare.

Your Resume as a Selling Tool

The single most important function of your resume is to sell you. In many instances, your resume will arrive at a prospective employer's door before you do. It will determine in large part whether you get an interview for the job you are seeking.

Even if you have met a prospective employer at a party or some other event and engaged him in a conversation that led to a request for your resume, a poorly done resume can ruin the possibility of a job. So it is all too easy to imagine how quickly you can lose in the resume game if you send a poorly done resume to someone who has never even laid eyes on you.

How do you write a resume that presents you in your best light? First, it must be well-organized. It must look good and be graphically pleasing to the eye. It must contain all the necessary information about you. It must sell you as a serious job candidate with many qualifications and skills to offer an employer.

A Well-Organized Resume A resume must be well-organized. This not only means that what you write must be carefully thought out but also that the overall design and format must be pleasing to the eye and logically arranged on the page. Chapter 2 goes into detail about the physical appearance of your resume and how to plan it. Chapters 4 and 5 will help you cull information about yourself and then actually write a resume that describes you and shows you off.

These combined elements should produce a well-organized resume that shows you have organizational skills—and a person who can condense a lifetime's worth of work and education into one to three pages will undoubtedly impress an employer as someone who is capable of organizing a much larger work project.

WHAT GOES INTO A RESUME

A resume must contain a certain amount of essential information. Although this information varies from person to person, several categories are standard in any resume:

1. A heading, which may be as simple as the word "Resume" at the top of the page or as complicated as a well-thought-out "Job Objective" that describes the type of position you hope to obtain
2. Your name, address, city, state, and phone numbers where you can be reached
3. A job title or objective if that was not part of the title and if that applies to the type of work you seek
4. A detailed record of your employment history
5. A detailed record of your education
6. Any languages you know
7. Anything you have published, either magazine or journal articles or books, if this is pertinent to the work you do
8. Any relevant professional memberships
9. A record of your military service
10. Any personal information you feel is important and choose to include
11. A statement to the effect that your references and any samples of your work, if that applies to the kind of work you do, are available on request

The descriptions that follow are the maximum number of items that would appear on a resume. Few persons will choose to use all these categories. Knowing which categories you should choose is part of the knack of resume writing.

Let's take a look at each of these items in greater detail.

The Heading. In many instances, as already noted, the heading of your resume can simply be the word "Resume." Or you might write "Resume of [fill in your name]." Some persons choose to use their name as the heading for the resume; others use a job title or objective. The point is that there should be some identifying line at the top of the resume—some clue to the reader that lets him know what he is about to read.

If most of your resumes will be going to contacts, your name may be the best heading. If most of your resumes will be going to unknown personnel directors, a job title may be the best approach.

Name, Address, Phone Numbers. Your name, address, city, state, and phone numbers may seem too irrelevant to mention, but this information is vital—and too often forgotten. The personnel director of a Fortune 500 company reported his frustration at receiving the perfect resume from what appeared to be the perfectly qualified candidate for a very high-level management position—only to discover that it contained no name or address. Failing to include your name and address is a fatal mistake—no one can call you or write you to tell you that you omitted it. Also, it is important to include your zip code and telephone area code if you will be applying for jobs out of your state or community.

Deciding what telephone number to put on your resume can pose a problem. Obviously, you will not be in a position to take many calls about job possibilities while you are at work. In fact, some employers have admitted to being hesitant about hiring someone who can talk for hours during the work day. Possibly the best solution is to list your present office number and your home number. When you are called during the day, keep the call as brief as possible and ask if you can call back during the evening or your lunch hour. No one expects you to jeopardize your present job for a future one, so most prospective employers will be understanding and cooperative about making arrangements for you to call back. Also, the presence of your home phone indicates that you can be reached after work hours. Most of the callers responding to your resume will be prepared to save most of the talking for the interview and will expect only a brief telephone conversation to set up the interview, particularly if they have called you at work.

Job Title or Objective. Most resumes need either a job title or a job objective. A job title, if you choose to use one, should be a simple one- or two-word description of what you do—speech therapist, technical writer, paramedic. A job title usually reflects your present level of skills rather than what you hope to do next. The one excep-

3

tion is the job title for a new college graduate, who should, of course, note what he or she hopes to do. Putting "College Graduate" down as a job title would be silly.

If you are hoping to make a sizable jump in responsibilities, a job objective may be more appropriate for your resume. A job objective also works well for a college graduate seeking an entry-level position. It should be used, in short, when you feel you would like to do a little more explaining about your needs. A job objective can be less defining than a job title, or it can be very specific about stating what you hope to obtain in your next position. If, for example, you are job hunting in a favorable job market, you may want a fairly open, vague job objective that will cause employers to consider you for a variety of jobs. Still, not every resume must have a job objective. If you find that your job objective is too vague to be useful, do not include it.

In a tight job market, you might do better to write a more specific job objective—one that is geared exactly to the job you know you want. Specialists and highly trained technicians generally do better with a fairly specific job objective; if you fall into this category, the range of work you do is fairly well defined, and there is little point in leaving yourself open to positions that you have no intention of filling.

A job objective should be clearly labeled as such. It should be concise and definitive, and probably should not run more than three to five lines. Examples of job objectives appear on resumes throughout this book.

Employment Record.   After the job title comes your employment record. There are several ways to write this, depending upon the type of resume format you choose. You could begin with your most recent job and work back to the first, or first relevant, position. Or you could describe the work you have done or your accomplishments in one section and give a brief chronology in another section. This is a technique favored by over-forty managerial persons and persons who are looking for a first job—in each case, age might be held against the person, so achievements are stressed before the chronology is presented.

Your resume must include the dates of your employment. If it does not, many personnel workers will toss it out. Also, if possible, give the exact dates of each employment; include the days if you can, but definitely give the month and year, or the years alone if you have worked for many years. If one item is consistently checked on a resume, it is the dates of employment, and it is not worth the risk to misrepresent them.

If there are gaps in your employment record due to illness or unemployment, there is no reason to try to cover them up. Simply omit these years on the resume and explain them honestly if they are brought up during an interview.

You need not give a description of every job you have ever held, particularly if you have worked for a long time. As you gain more experience, list only the jobs that are relevant. A prospective employer reads a resume to see what you have been doing, not where you have been doing it.

Education. After your employment record comes your educational background. If you are a professional, begin with your most recent education. If you stopped attending school after high school, list your high school first.

A good guideline in describing your education is to give the most details about the schooling that most directly applies to the position you hope to obtain. A person holding a doctorate in American history needs to mention only the name of his high school and the year of graduation. Far more important are his academic credentials beyond high school. A graduate of a vocational school should give the greater share of space to describing his vocational training and should not include many details of his high school education.

Generally, begin with your most recent educational experience and work your way backward in time.

Grade standing, unless important to your career field, need not be mentioned. But law-school graduates, for example, are expected to mention class standing on a resume. A literature major need not. You certainly should not mention class standing if it will not work in your favor.

School honors and organizations, too, need not be mentioned unless they are important to your career.

A recent graduate would be more inclined to mention academic honors or extracurricular activities, because they are all he has to sell. As work experience is gained, such items should be dropped from the resume.

If you have taken or are taking night-school courses to update your skills, they are important to mention on a resume, as are seminars, workshops, conferences, and other career-related educational activities you may be involved in.

Languages. After education, note any languages that you know and the level of proficiency.

Publications. In some fields, notably academia, published works are important and should be noted on a resume. Go for quality rather than quantity, however, if you have published a great deal. Too many academic resumes run on for pages listing publications— so many, in fact, that it soon becomes apparent that lots of graduate students had to be helping out. Far better simply to state that you have published *x* number of articles and to list a few of the more impressive journals in which you are published than to detail 200 articles published over the past ten years.

Academic credits should include the title of the work, publishers, date of publication, and city of publication. Journal or magazine articles include a volume number and issue date, if noted on the publication. A good stylebook contains details on writing a publishing credit note.

5

Professional Memberships.   Mention only those memberships that are directly relevant to your work skills. Community or church participation are no longer considered pertinent items to include on a resume. Do not go into great detail about these activities, or you may give the impression that your after-work activities could cut into your work hours.

Military Service.   List the branch of service, dates of service, rank at time of discharge, and briefly state what you did in the service.

Personal Information.   Personal information is a little tricky these days. Legally, prospective employers can ask you very little about yourself, and you do not have to supply any personal information such as marital status, plans regarding children, or age. One subtle way to exchange this information, however, is to put it on a resume. On the other hand, if your age might work against you, why announce it in advance? Obviously, once you are on an interview, the interviewer can readily judge your age. But if you write an otherwise sound resume with no mention of your age, you may have a better chance of getting the interview.

A good rule of thumb is to include the bare minimum of personal information that will be required for you to obtain an interview.

If you are comfortable including personal information, the most you will probably want to include is your birth date (not your age, which changes every year), willingness to relocate, and willingness to travel. Obviously, no mention should be made of the fact that you are not willing to relocate or travel.

Too many persons include too much information about their families. The names and ages of your children will not help you get a job, for example, nor will a listing of your wife's accomplishments.

Other personal information you include in your resume should have a direct bearing on the work you hope to do. If you are applying for work with an international firm and you have lived in Spain and are fluent in two languages besides English, for example, this is personal information that definitely should be included.

References and Portfolio.   The final section of your resume is a formality—a statement that you will and can supply references if and when the job looks definite enough for a prospective employer to start checking out these things. Persons who work in creative fields should also be prepared to present samples of their work, often referred to as a portfolio.

Arranging the Information

The order of these categories of information will vary from resume to resume. Usually it appears in the order in which it was just described. If your academic credentials are very important, though, you might continue to present them ahead of work history for several years.

Personal information might appear right after your name and address or at the very end of the resume. These are questions of choice that relate more to the look of the resume and the actual information than to any arbitrary way of doing things.

Generally, when listing work experience and education, begin with your most recent experience.

Because it is so important not to omit any pertinent information, a checklist of the categories of information is included in chapter 5. Use it for the final check when you have finished writing your resume and before you have it professionally typed.

2 MAKING YOUR RESUME LOOK GOOD

Editors and typographers have long been aware that some combinations of words on a printed page look more attractive than others do. While it is impossible to develop the keen eye of a typographer without training, you can follow a few guidelines for organizing the way a resume looks to ensure that it will be pleasing to the eye of the reader.

RESUME STYLES

There are two widely accepted kinds of resumes. The most common kind—and the one most useful to personnel persons—is the historical-chronological resume. In this type of resume, you present your work and educational histories in chronological order, beginning with your most recent experience.

Even if you have decided to use the other form for your resume, it is probably a good idea to prepare a chronological resume, simply because it provides a good basis for any spin-off resumes you may want to write.

Remember, too, that the chronological resume merely puts the dates in your life up front; all other resumes must also contain the times when you worked in various places and when you attended school. Resumes without this vital information are often discarded without even one serious reading. On page 33 is an example of a historical-chronological resume.

The second widely accepted type of resume is the skills- or achievement-oriented resume. It emphasizes skills and achievement above chronological events.

9

RESUME FORMATS

The format of a resume refers to how it looks physically. A great deal of thought must be given to the physical arrangement of a resume. It should be easy to read, compact, and preferably not more than two pages. If you are having difficulty fitting what you have to say into this number of pages, you may be trying to say too much. Go over the information one more time to see if there is anything else you can take out.

Leave a sizable margin—one to one and a half inches—all around. Single space the resume and double- or triple-space between categories of information. Because a single-spaced copy is sometimes hard to read, try to organize all the type in your resume carefully to ensure that it is easy to read and attractive to the eye. Study the examples that follow. Which ones look least cluttered to you? Which resume has the most pleasing appearance?

Resume 1 is the most pleasing to the eye, because it follows standard guidelines used by graphic designers and typesetters to organize type for magazines, books, and other printed materials. The white margins are equal on the top and two sides and slightly larger at the bottom. Identical heads are used to introduce parallel sections of information. It also makes the most efficient use of space.

Resume 2 won't hurt the reader's eyes, but it does waste valuable space that might better be put to use selling your job skills. This is a popular format and actually works fairly well for a one-page resume. If your resume tends to run long or if you have a lot to say, you may want to avoid this format.

Resume 3 is cluttered looking. The margins are too small; the arrangement of type on the page appears to follow no set pattern. Initially, subheads are aligned with the left margin; then they are in the center of the page. All in all, this is a messy-looking resume, better avoided.

A resume should be written on white or pale-colored bond paper or other paper of good quality. Pale colors are less conservative than white, but they are acceptable in most places. Buff, light brown, manila, and pale gray are colors you may choose from. Probably the best reason for using colored paper is that it coordinates with your stationery. But in most conservative fields, such as banking, business, and law, white paper is still safest.

A resume should be printed on paper 8½ by 11 inches. It should be at least twenty-pound weight so as not to appear skimpy. Go to heavier paper—up to sixty-pound—if your resume is one-page long. A resume that runs two or three pages should be on lighter-weight paper or mailing it will become a problem; you will find yourself spending money for extra postage and buying large envelopes. Sometimes resumes are printed on copy-machine paper; this is fine if the paper is high enough in quality.

1

2

3

Try to draw a rough sketch of your resume once you have culled enough information so that you can begin to visualize how you might arrange it. The resume may turn out different when you actually type it, but drawing such a sketch will give you an idea where copy blocks should go and how much space to allot for everything.

Using Headlines to Divide the Resume

To plan the format of your resume, decide what headlines or identification lines you will need. The most obvious head you will need is the word "Resume" or your name in bold type. Sometimes "Vita" or "Curriculum Vitae" is used instead of "Resume,' but this is done mostly by academics. This is the major head, and it should stand out more than any other head on the page. You will probably want to put it in capital letters or in capital letters and small letters with underlining.

Draw up a list of other heads you will need—usually these include Education, Work History or Employment, Personal, Honors or Professional Honors, Publications, and Military Service. These heads are all similar—that is, they introduce blocks of descriptive copy—so they should all be identical. You can choose to underline them, capitalize them, put them flush left or right or center them on the page; just make sure that they are all exactly alike and in the same position.

Organizing Information Blocks

The next step is to organize the information blocks that will go under the heads. Anything not used to label a section is an information block; the information blocks are the paragraphs that contain data about your education, work history, and so on.

They should be organized to look as much alike as possible. There will be some problems: for example, the sections on your employment history and your education will contain dates, whereas the personal-information section and the professional-honors section may not. Just remember that the dates must be done in exactly the same way in all sections with dates.

Information blocks may be written in paragraph form as follows:

October 1955-June 1961, ABC Company

After a six-month training period, I went to work in the department responsible for purchasing machine parts. I was promoted to assistant buyer for machine parts in 1958. In 1959, I assumed direction of all buying for company.

Information blocks may be organized into lists, as follows:

1963-1967   Duke University, B.A., literature
1967-1969   Indiana University, M.A., cultural anthropology

These two examples show several points you need to consider when planning your resume. First, decide whether you want information blocks indented and if so, how much they will be indented. You can also decide what kind of indents you want. You can indent the first line three to five spaces, as follows:

> Established new approaches, systems, and procedures in product development at ABC Publishing Company. Developed a step-by-step approach to planning...

You can use a hanging indent, in which the first line is flush left and the remaining lines are indented, as follows:

> Established new approaches, systems, and procedures in product development at ABC Publishing Company. Developed a step-by-step approach to planning...

Or you can decide not to indent at all and to use extra space to separate the paragraphs. Whatever you do, be consistent—do exactly the same thing to every paragraph.

Second, decide whether you want to use periods at the end of information blocks. Since complete sentences usually end with periods, the answer is nearly always yes. But if you have several lists that are not complete sentences, you should omit periods. Here is an example of a list where periods would be silly:

> <u>Skills</u>
>
> IBM Selectric typewriter—80 w.p.m.
> Pitman shorthand
> Dictaphone
> Adding machine
> Office calculator

Try to keep information blocks similar in size. If one does run longer than the others, it should be the one describing your most recent position. Detailed descriptions of early jobs should gradually be pared down as you gain more experience.

Once you have decided what goes into each information block, how you will indent it, and whether you will use periods at the end, decide whether you want to emphasize anything within the block. In your employment section, for example, you will probably want to emphasize the title of the jobs you have held, as follows:

> December 1958-November 1963   Senior editor

Or you might write:

> Senior editor, Olympia Publishing, 1958-1963

The best way to add emphasis within an information block is to underline; capital letters are too strong.

Be careful about adding too much emphasis, though. Most people make that mistake in a resume. Underline only those words or numbers that you truly want to stand out—those items that are very important to you and to a prospective employer.

The best way to learn about resume formats is to study other resumes. Look through the resumes in this book for ideas on the format of your resume. Gradually you will develop an eye for what looks pleasing on the printed page and what looks messy.

3 MODEL RESUMES

Resumes are highly personal, and you will not be able to copy a resume from this book for your own use. By reading all the resumes carefully, however, you may obtain hints on how to write a resume or even a particular paragraph that has been troubling you.

Each resume is titled with the kind of job that is described in that resume. At the end of almost every resume is a brief list of other jobs for which that resume could be used.

MASTER RESUME INDEX

ACCOUNTANT-AUDITOR

RESUME OF MARY DALEY   CERTIFIED PUBLIC ACCOUNTANT

1288 Shortridge Drive
Raleigh, North Carolina 27605
222-1597

Will travel   Will relocate

JOB OBJECTIVE

Position as comptroller for small- to middle-sized services-oriented firm.

WORK EXPERIENCE

Treasurer, GHI Products, Inc., Columbus, North Carolina. 1972 to present.
In addition to my usual responsibilities as treasurer, I have reorganized
the billing system, which has resulted in an annual savings of $35,000 to
the firm.

Manager of internal auditing, HHH Insurance Co., Hillside, South Carolina.
1968 to 1972. Responsible for seven corporate accounts. Supervised staff
of eighteen. Instituted new office procedures to eliminate paperwork and
save time for staff.

Internal auditor, senior level, HHH Insurance Co. 1967 to 1968.

Internal auditor, trainee, HHH Insurance Co. 1965 to 1967.

EDUCATION and HONORS

B.A., accounting, Johnsville State University, Johnsville, South Carolina,
1967.

Became Certified Public Accountant, 1973.

Member of Financial Women's Executives Association; served as vice president in charge of membership.

REFERENCES

Available on request.

**Bank executive, financial manager,
internal auditor, public
accountant, tax accountant**

ADVERTISING ASSISTANT — New Graduate

MARGIE RUBENSTEIN

123 Evans Avenue   Available after May 16, 1979
Iowa City, Iowa 52242   1001 Eighteenth Avenue
(319) 348-6666   (515) 858-3174

JOB OBJECTIVE:
Advertising-assistant position with possible advancement to a career as
an account executive.

EDUCATION:
B.A., May 1979, University of Iowa. Concentrations in Journalism and
Marketing. Earned 50% of college expenses.

Course Highlights: Marketing Communications, Consumer Behavior, Theory/
Practice of Persuasion, Advertising Theory/Planning, News Editing,
Graphic Arts, Organizing Mass Communication Productions.

EXPERIENCE:
Advertising and Reporting: Advertising Intern (Summer 1978), Sun
Newspapers of Omaha. Responsibilities were handling and servicing
various account departments, the advertising director's accounts,
designing and laying out ads, selling ad space, and working in traffic
control. Feature Reporter (Summer 1977), Eldora Herald Index. Wrote
feature articles, covered city council meetings, set headlines, sold
and laid out advertising for a special insert. Stencil Designer
(Summer 1975, 1976), Dodger Gym Manufacturing. Designed in-house
stencils for customer orders and stenciled athletic wear. Standing
job with Dodger Gym for all semester and spring breaks.

Other Work Experience: Hostess/Waitress, Shipping Department, Crew Boss.

PUBLICATIONS/PROJECTS:
Feature stories, Eldora Herald Index; two articles, School of Journalism
Lab Tabs; editor of a four-page tabloid; editor of a marketing-research
analysis project for Hardee's; advertisements, Eldora Herald Index and
the Sun Newspapers; now in progress, twenty-minute documentary in film.

HONORS/AWARDS:
University of Iowa athletic scholarship, scholarship loan from Miriam
Brown Educational Trust Fund, Dolphin Queen candidate.

Advertising Copywriter, media
trainee   (Continued)

COLLEGE ACTIVITIES:
Member/team captain of Women's Intercollegiate Basketball Team, intra-
mural athletics, selected member of Greek Expansion Task Force, publica-
tions/historian Pi Beta Phi, March of Dimes Fund Drive.

PERSONAL:
Single; 22; no geographical preference.

Strengths: energetic, work well under pressure, very willing to accept
responsibility, have great perseverance.

REFERENCES/PORTFOLIO:
References available at Career Services and Placement Center, Iowa
Memorial Union, University of Iowa, Iowa City, Iowa 52242,
(319) 353-3147. Portfolio available upon request.

AIRLINE RESERVATIONIST

R E S U M E

O F

A L I C E   O D E L L

I have two years experience as a reservationist on a major domestic air-line, a pleasant appearance, a personality that works well with the public, and a good speaking voice.

I am seeking a position with an international airlines as a ticket agent. Additional details about my skills and education are listed below. If you believe I am the person you are looking for, won't you test my speaking voice by calling

405-738-9386

WORK EXPERIENCE

August 1976-present. Employed with United Airlines as a phone reservationist for twelve months. For past twelve months, I have worked as a ticket agent in a major downtown travel center, where I handle off-the-street traffic as well as phone inquiries about travel plans.

CAREER TRAINING

One-week training course at professional airlines school in Tallahassee, Florida.

Four weeks on-the-job training by United Airlines.

One-week seminar on "Using Computers in Reservations Work."

EDUCATION

Associate degree, Truman Junior College, Chicago, Illinois, June 1976.

Graduated Eden High School, Chicago, Illinois, June 1974.

PERSONAL INTERESTS

Travel, championship swimmer in high school and college, reading, sewing.

43 East Eighty-third Street, New York, New York   10022

Airline flight attendant,
reservations clerk, travel agent

ART DIRECTOR

WALTER JUSTIN

1190 Gulf Lane   Phone: 312-756-7309
Park Ridge, Illinois   60068   312-744-7590

JOB OBJECTIVE

Position as senior art director in large urban advertising agency.

CAPSULE

My primary activity as art director has been to supervise the creative
work on various advertising projects. I have carried as many as ten
accounts at one time and have worked on five major cigarette accounts
(at various times), one car account, and two major cosmetic accounts.
Responsibilities include: hiring and working with layout artists, copywriters, and designers, and supervising an in-house creative team. In
all the accounts I have handled, I have been a primary force in generat-
ing and developing advertising ideas, and I consider the ability to do
this one of my major strengths.

CHRONOLOGICAL RECORD

J. Christopher Agency, 1975-present. Hired as assistant art director
when this agency was less than one year old, I have progressed to art
director and the agency has tripled in size and become an important
force in the advertising world.

EDUCATION

Art Institute of Chicago, B.A., fine arts, 1973.
Lived in Paris, France, studied at Sorbonne, 1974.

PORTFOLIO AND REFERENCES

Available on request.

*Advertising assistant, advertising
executive, advertising media buyer,
advertising production manager,
freelance artist, media manager*

BANK TELLER

MARGARET EBERT
8380 Green Avenue, S.W.
Washington, D.C. 20023
Phone: 202-837-8291

Job Title

Bank Teller

Work Experience

Commercial Teller

First Federal Savings & Loan
Washington, D.C.
October 1973-Present
Three weeks special training in
use of computer terminal.

Assistant Note Teller

National Boulevard Bank
Washington, D.C.
April 1972-October 1973

Education

Saugatauk Junior College, one year, business administration
Saugatauk High School, graduated January 1972. Took business curriculum.

Interests

People, music, reading, travel

*Accounting trainee, accounts-
receivable clerk, billing clerk, note
teller*

BOOKKEEPER

Accounting Clerk

Victoria Taylor
600 Mill Road
Hyattsville, Maryland 20782
Phone: 958-9584

Employment Record

Statements Clerk
H.M. Sanders, Accountants, 1976 to present

Major responsibility: preparing periodic statements reports for four major clients. Also assist with internal auditing for these firms.

Bookkeeper
Henderson, Inc., 1975-1976

Responsible for wide variety of functions: maintaining ledger records, accounts receivable on daily sales, payroll deductions, some routine clerical work such as typing vouchers, invoices, and other records. Was hired as a secretary to operations vice president, promoted to bookkeeper after four months.

Education

Delaware Junior College, associate degree in business and bookkeeping, 1975
Delaware Central High School, business course, graduated 1973.

Skills

Familiar with most accounting-related business machines
Typing
Shorthand

Personal

Married, divorced, no children
Will relocate, will travel

Accounting trainee, accounts-receivable clerk, billing clerk, file clerk, hospital billing clerk

CARPENTER

Tom MacFarlane
1930 Clinton Avenue East
San Jose, New Mexico 87565
Phone: 328-0070

Summary

Seek employment as carpenter; have extensive training and am capable of either rough or finished work. Specialize in building new houses.

Job Training

Apprentice in Carpenters' Program, sponsored by local union. Involved four years of on-the-job training plus 144 hours of classroom instruction. 1952-1956.

Hightower Architectural Company. Worked two years in drafting and blueprint reading. 1950-1951.

Mountain Black High School. Vocational course in carpentry. Each year the senior class built a house as its project. I served as carpentry foreman. 1946-1950.

Job Experience

Worked various construction sites, 1956 to present. For past six years, have worked as carpenters' foreman for Grimstead Construction, San Ildefonso, New Mexico.

References

Furnished on request.

Building-trades worker, electrician, construction foreman, supervisor, tool and die maker

CASHIER

RESUME

Suzanne Goodman   893 Eaton Place
Phone: 938-8371   Onawa, Maine 04470

JOB OBJECTIVE: Cashier in grocery store or other retail store

WORK HISTORY: Cash and Carry Department Store
                Chicago, Illinois
                April 1973 to present

                Sloan's Vegetable Mart
                Chicago, Illinois
                August 1972-April 1973

                Pay Less Groceries
                Chicago, Illinois
                Part-time while attending high school
                September 1968-June 1972

SKILLS: Familiar with optical and magnetic scanner
                Familiar with all office functions of grocery
                  store, such as exchange forms, change forms,
                  receipts
                Familiar with adding machine
                Familiar with point-of-change terminals

EDUCATION: Knob Hill High School
                Graduated June 1972
                Studied business and office-skills course

REFERENCES: Available on request

Bank teller, retail salesperson

CHEF

RESUME

Mark Jones
800 Mountain Drive   Phones: 487-1100 (home)
San Francisco, California 94102   555-4444 (office)

Job Objective: Position as dessert chef in kitchen of restaurant recognized for standards of excellence in food preparation.

Employment: Sauce and dessert chef, alternate shifts, Mountainside View Resort, since 1976.

Chief lunch chef, ABC Quik Foods, Inc., Oregon City, 1974-1976.

Junior dessert chef, Whitesides Hotel, Chicago, 1971-1974.

Education: Oregon City Vocational High School program for
professional cooking and restaurant management, graduated
January 1971.

Personal: Will travel; will relocate; would be particularly
interested in metropolitan area.

*Counter/short-order cook, food
services worker, restaurant
manager*

COMMERCIAL ARTIST

David Eaves
444 Riverside Lane
Kansas City, Kansas 66106
Telephone: 837-8371

SUMMARY

Commercial artist specializing in finished illustration, known for cartoon style.

WORK EXPERIENCE

August 1973 to present, Gotham Advertising Agency, Chicago, Illinois. Rough-sketch artist and layout person.

September 1970 to August 1973. Freelance children's book illustrator, Chicago, Illinois.

June 1968 to August 1970, Bloom Art Studio, Chicago, Illinois. Responsibilities included artwork through rough layout to finished design for major advertising campaigns for women's beauty-care product line, food manufacturer's customer-use booklets, and a variety of individual illustrations sold to clients. Cartoon style was fully developed during this stage and became my professional signature.

EDUCATION

Rhode Island School of Design, 1966 to 1968. Studied commercial illustration.

Boone Commercial High School, Kansas City, Kansas. Graduated June 1966. Studied vocational course in commercial art.

INTERESTS

Illustrating children's books.

PERSONAL

Single   Born 7-2-48
Will relocate   Good health

*Art director, art production
manager, freelance artist, graphic-
arts salesperson, layout artist*

31

COMPUTER PROGRAMMER

Nancy Edelman

Computer Programmer

Job Objective

Position as lead programmer with supervisory responsibilities.

Work History

1972-present   Senior programmer. Computron Electronics, Inc.
                Primary task was to convert tabulating and bookkeeping
                systems for three major clients to computer programs
                and to write reports recommending hardware they would
                require.

1967-1972   Programmer. Datatronics, Inc. Four weeks of intensive
                classroom and on-the-job training prepared me to take
                on responsibilities as full-time programmer. Was in-
                volved in creating programs and checking programs of
                others.

Education

1963-1967   B.S., data processing and accounting, Tri-State College.
                Have attended four seminars since graduation to update
                myself on software and new technology.

1959-1963   Green Mountain High School, graduated with honors.

Personal
5187 Arlington Drive
Nashville, Tennessee 37212
Phone: 594-8900
Single; excellent health
Will relocate

References furnished on request.

*Computer operator, computer
programmer, data processor,
keypunch operator, systems analyst*

COPYWRITER

Rowena Dunne

OBJECTIVE

Copywriting position in which I can use my expertise in food marketing.

WORK HISTORY

1972-present   Senior Copywriter, Burton Advertising.
Chief copywriter on five major food accounts, responsible
for two monthly magazines published by clients, one newsletter, and several miscellaneous reports and booklets
geared to the consumer market. Wrote a cookbook for a major
client in 1975.

1970-1972   Copywriter, International Food Advertisers, Inc.
Wrote wide variety of copy for booklets, advertisements, and
brochures describing various food products. Clients included Egg Council and three manufacturers of prepared foods.

1968-1970   Administrative assistant and researcher, Food, Inc., a con-
cern that published three monthly magazines geared to the
food industry. In addition to my secretarial responsibilities, I gradually began to research articles and write
brief pieces for these publications.

EDUCATION

1968, B.A., Blackson University, liberal arts.
1966, associate's degree, Seabrook Junior College, liberal arts.
Have taken various night-school courses:

      Copywriting, Indiana University Extension
      Business Law, Indiana University Extension
      Business Administration and Marketing, Advertiser's Institute
      Marketing Strategies, Advertiser's Institute

PERSONAL

Phone: 888-0907
Married, three children
Health, excellent
139 Seabrook Lane
Oceanview, California 94586

References and samples available on request.

*Writer, direct-mail writer, house-
organ editor, press agent,
procedure writer, technical writer*

CREDIT MANAGER

CINDY THOMAN
142 Lake Drive
Indianapolis, Indiana 46259
Phone: 472-3381

Job Objective   Position as credit manager of retail clothing store or
in department-store credit department.

Personal   Married, one school-age child.
Willing to relocate in any major Midwestern city.

Work Experience

July 1978
to
present

Assistant Credit Manager for XXX Corporation, the credit
division of a retail clothing store, located in Lima,
Ohio.
Assisted customers in filling out applications for
credit, checked credit references, and wrote report
regarding granting of credit. Worked closely with
credit agencies when customer was under consideration
for credit. Reviewed and passed on credit-agency
reports. When credit manager took a two-month leave,
I assumed responsibility for twelve-person office,
managing work of clerks, typists, and bookkeepers.

October 1970
to
June 1978

Trainee in First Federal Bank's program for recent
college graduates. Worked various assignments as bookkeeper, collection teller, and loan-approval trainee.
Promoted in January 1972 to Junior Loan Officer. Major
responsibility was to help customers complete applications for loans, check credit references, and report
recommendation to board of vice presidents, who made
decision about granting loan.

Education   Graduated from University High School, Bloomington,
Indiana, June 1966. B.A. from Purdue University, 1970;
major, economics; minor, business administration.

*Bank branch manager, collection
manager, commercial loan officer,
financial manager*

DENTAL ASSISTANT

DENTAL ASSISTANT

Beth LeBrun   3488 Stockton Drive
Phone: 763-8974   Waverly, New Mexico 87501

JOB OBJECTIVE: Position in dentist's office that includes
public contact and possibly some work in educating the public
to better dental practices. I feel that besides having the
skills necessary to function as a dental assistant, I have
teaching talents that I could contribute to any dentist's practice.

TRAINING: Mount Ryder Junior College, 1970. Awarded certificate in dental assisting. In addition to required courses, I
took typing, office management, and business accounting. High
school graduate, equivalency certificate awarded, 1968.

PROFESSIONAL: Certified as Dental Assistant by Certifying
Board of New Mexico.

WORK EXPERIENCE: Office of John Smithton, D.D.S., 1970 to
present. Responsibilities have included recordkeeping on
patient's health as well as billing, assisting dentist in preparing materials for making impressions and doing restoration
work, and exposing X-ray film. In 1975, I initiated a program
to teach dental hygiene to children. This program, which con-
sists of a fifteen-minute talk using a puppet, has become a
regular part of the office procedure for any patient under the
age of eight. I have fulfilled requests for me to give this
talk to various grade-school classes in the community.

REFERENCES: References and samples of work available on request.

Dental hygienist, dentist,
paramedic

DIETITIAN — New Graduate

RESUME

PERSONAL
Marvin Brye
1345 Brilton Lane
Norwich, Connecticut 06360
Phone: 888-8367
Single
Will relocate

EDUCATION
M.S., foods and nutrition, 1979
Cum laude
Connecticut State College

B.S., institutional management, 1977
Connecticut State College

WORK
EXPERIENCE
Internship, Connecticut State Hospital and
    Nursing Home Facility, 1978
Internship was divided into rotating services.
I elected to work in gerontology, patient diet
education, meal service, and outpatient coun-
seling.

For four summers, I also worked at the Connecticut State Nursing Home Facility as a junior
chef and during the last year as a diet counselor.

HONORS
Registered dietitian

PUBLICATIONS
Author of article, "The Role of Education in the
Diet of Persons over Seventy," published in
National Hospital Dietitian.

REFERENCES
References and copy of article available on
request.

Dietitian, nutritionist

DOCTOR'S ASSISTANT

Bernard Wharton
5198 Fifty-fifth Street
Cleveland, Ohio 44122
Phone: 870-3173

Job Objective   Position as doctor's assistant; private or small
                     clinical practice preferred.

Work History   Cleveland City Hospital. 1973-present. Worked as
                     paramedic in emergency, surgery, and psychiatric
                     services. Involved in routine patient care, assisted
                     with medical examinations and minor surgery, dispensed
                     medicine on psychiatric ward, and worked with group
                     therapy.

Education   Cleveland City College, 1971-1973.
                     Paramedical course, included part-time internship at
                     Cleveland City Hospital.
                     Cleveland City High School, 1963-1967.

Military   U.S. Army, 1967-1971. Trained as paramedic. Stationed
                     in Saigon. Honorable discharge with rank of specialist.

References   Furnished on request.

Laboratory technician, paramedic

DRAFTER — New Graduate of Vocational School

```
                        RESUME OF

                      EDWARD BISHOP




PERSONAL        Single                   400 Drivers Lane
                Will relocate            Chicago, Illinois
                Born December 12, 1959   312-355-0056



EDUCATION       Graduated spring 1979 from Industrial Design
                Institute after completing two-year course in
                drafting.  Awarded associate degree.

                Graduated spring 1977 from Acton Vocational
                High School.  Took four years each of physical
                science, drafting, and industrial design.



SUMMER WORK     Worked construction projects for past four
                summers.  Achieved junior rank as carpenter.



JOB OBJECTIVE   Beginner's position in middle-size architectural
                firm as tracer.
```

Architect, mechanical artist

ECONOMIST

Joan McElroy   Will relocate
4560 Endview Lane   Will travel
Palo Alto, California 94300
Phone: 405-566-7603

Job Objective

Seeking research position in government agency. Areas of specialty: crop
forecasting, price-wage index evaluation.

Employment History

Blackwell Insurance Agency, Riverside, Montana
October 1971-May 1973
Actuary assistant
Worked primarily as staff statistician, compiling actuarial tables based
on absenteeism.

First Federal Bank, Riverside, Montana
May 1973-present
Statistician
Responsible for ongoing review of wheat-crop forecasts prepared by junior
statisticians. Supervised staff of two.

Education

Graduated from Montana State University
B.A. in public economics; minor in business administration, January 1973

Am currently attending night school. Anticipate receiving master's degree
in economics in June 19__.

*Budget analyst, comptroller,
economic analyst, financial analyst,
financial forecaster, statistician*

EDITOR

Rosemary Smith
536 Brompton, Apt. 3-S
Chicago, Illinois 60657
Telephone: (Residence) 312/472-3882 (Office) 312/267-6868, Ext. 570

OBJECTIVES

To be a project editor in a college or elementary/high school department.
My major fields of competence and interest are Modern Languages, Education,
Social Sciences, and Humanities.

SUMMARY

I have been an editor in textbook publishing for over ten years. Currently,
I am a project editor at Randolph College Publishing Co., where I am in
charge of coordinating three college-level French projects and am responsible for supervising the personnel involved. These projects are comprised
of ten components: two texts, two readers, two workbooks, two instructor's
manuals, and two sets of tapes. In addition to coordinating and supervising, I am involved in editing, production, and product development. Prior
to being a project editor, I was a manuscript editor at Jackson Publishing
for college-level French, education, and psychology texts. My duties as a
manuscript editor involved copyediting, content editing, production, and
working with designers, artists, authors, and typesetters. I entered
publishing as an editor in the elementary/high school department of Elementary School Plus Publishing Co., where my duties consisted mainly of
writing, rewriting, and doing some production and design work. I have two
years of teaching experience at the eighth- and ninth-grade levels. I have
a Magistere degree in French, an M.A.T. degree in French/Education, and a
B.A. degree in French and music.

EMPLOYMENT HISTORY

Dates	Title	Institution	Location
present-3/76	Project Editor (college)	Randolph College Publishing Co.	New York
2/76-4/73	Manuscript Editor (college)	Randolph College Publishing Co.	New York
3/73-9/69	Editor (el/high)	Elementary School Plus Publishing Co.	New York
6/69-9/67	French Teacher	Easton Junior High School	Watertown, Massachusetts

Acquisitions editor, freelance editor, house-organ editor, journalist, junior editor, photojournalist, senior editor, trade journalist

(Continued)

40

EDUCATION

Dates	School	Location	Major Fields	Degree
9/66-6/67	Sorbonne	Paris, France	French	Magistere (cum laude)
9/65-8/66	Brown University	Providence, R.I.	French/Education	M.A.T.
9/61-6/65	Randolph-Macon Woman's College	Lynchburg, Va.	Music/French	B.A.
9/58-6/61	York Community High School	Elmhurst, Ill.	College Prep.	Diploma

PRODUCT-DEVELOPMENT EXPERIENCE

I have surveyed and analyzed competitive texts, conducted telephone surveys of instructors, solicited written critiques, and prepared guidelines for revision in planning new editions and developing new texts.

SKILLS AND ABILITIES

Editing Skills
copyediting, content editing, writing, rewriting, proofreading, working with authors and sponsoring editors

Production Skills
manuscript markup; page layout; experience with photos, line art, design, audio tapes

Managerial Skills
supervisory skills, budget control, scheduling

Background Abilities
teaching experience, fluency in French

Strong Points
rewriting, selecting visuals, dealing with authors, planning and organizing, meeting deadlines, staying within budgets, getting the best talent involved, shaping books to market needs. The books I edited have sold well.

ENVIRONMENTAL HEALTH INSPECTOR

A. Coleman Noyes II

4077 Coolidge Drive   Phone: 332-1040
Apartment 3
Littleton, Colorado   80120

Job Objective:

Position in environmental control with state or federal agency.

Work History:

Health inspector, Littleton Environmental Agency, 1975-present.
Responsibilities include examining suspected sites of pollution, con-
ducting laboratory tests, collecting routine air and water samples for
monthly testing.

Education:

B.S., University of Colorado, 1975.   Environmental health, major;
biology, minor.

Professional:

Licensed by State of Colorado

Personal:

Married, with four children
Will relocate

References:

Available on request.

Public administrator

EXECUTIVE SECRETARY

<u>Executive Secretary</u>

Martina Nunez
746 Cherry Drive
Logansport, Wyoming 82640
387-8455

<u>Work Experience</u>

1975-present. Connors Manufacturing. Secretary to vice president in charge of operations.

1970-1975. Film Masters, Inc. Secretary to executive vice president.

1962-1975. Mathews, Mathews, Targ, and Wolford, Counselors. Secretary to three senior partners in law firm specializing in corporate law.

1961-1962. Starlite Styrofoam Manufacturers, Inc. Responsibilities included general typing and light bookkeeping.

<u>Education</u>

1961. Dyer Secretarial School. Class standing: 4 out of 56.

<u>Skills</u>

Dictaphone
Shorthand--120 w.p.m.
Typing--90 w.p.m.

<u>References</u>

Will be furnished on request.

Administrative secretary, business-machine operator, general office worker, office manager

FILM EDITOR

Resume of

Jacqueline Remstadt

Personal   50 Mountain Laurel Drive
                San Jose, California 95100
                Phone: 487-9856 (home); 857-9905 (office)

Work   Freelance film editor, 1975 until present.
Experience
                Specialty: animation and short documentaries
                on subjects of interest to children and young
                adults.

                Paramount Studio, Hollywood, California,
                1962-1975. Edited full-length feature films.

                Independent Photographers' Union, San Jose,
                California, 1959-1962. Worked as photographer
                in industrial films; for first year was photog-
                rapher's assistant.

Education   San Jose Junior College, 1957-1958.
                Studied under Sam Reilly in film department.

References   Available.

Photographer, photojournalist

FREELANCE EDITOR

FREELANCE EDITOR

Brenda Thomas
433 South Lombard Avenue
Oak Park, IL 60302
312-348-0090

Education:

Completing M.A. in anthropology, Roosevelt University

Faculte de Medecin, Universite d'Aix-Marseille, Marseille, France,
1976-1977

B.A. with Honors in Anthropology, Roosevelt University, June 1974

Roosevelt University, Chicago, IL, 1972-1974

Harper College, Palatine, IL, 1970-1972

Skills:

Copyediting, rewriting, proofreading, cookbook editing

Clients:

Copyediting, proofreading-

> Nelson-Hall, Inc., 325 West Jackson, Chicago, IL 60606
> Law in American Society Foundation, 33 North LaSalle,
>   Chicago, IL 60602

Aldine Publishing Co., 529 South Wabash, Chicago, IL 60605

Copywriting-

Chemical Dynamics Corp., 4554 North Broadway, Chicago, IL 60611

References:

Will be furnished when requested.

*Senior editor, copyeditor, house-
organ editor, reporter*

GEOGRAPHER

Claude Trevor
3080 Eddy Street
Rockeville, Maryland 20014
487-9472

JOB OBJECTIVE

Teaching position with four-year university in geography-ecology department
with strong commitment to the field.

CAPSULE HISTORY

For the past five years, I have taught part-time at Northeastern Junior
College. I am the only instructor in geography and have organized and
developed the three courses I teach: Geography I, Ecology I and Ecology II.
In addition, I have held a full-time position as a geographer with the
State Department of Environmental Science. I have also worked as a com-
munity-development specialist and a site researcher.

CHRONOLOGICAL HISTORY

1974-present   Ecologist, State Department of Environmental Science.
                 Worked in soil and water testing and analysis.

                 Taught part-time at Northeastern Junior College.

1972-1974   Community Development Specialist, County Government. Did
                 site research for new developments and for communities plan-
                 ning physical expansion; checked that county criteria for
                 building, plumbing, and electricity installation were met.

1970-1972   G.S. Highon Manufacturing, producer of wood veneers. Worked
                 as site researcher; was primarily responsible for selection
                 of three tentative sites for new plant locations.

EDUCATION

1970   Ph.D., geography and environmental analysis, Western Science
                 University
1967   M.A., environmental science, All-State University
1966   B.A., geography (major), geology (minor), All-State University

PERSONAL

Divorced, no children
Will relocate

References available on request.

*Demographer, metallurgist,
physicist, professor, zoologist*

HOME ECONOMIST

LOLA BUCHANAN
30 Maple Drive
Dallas, Texas 75206
Phone: 862-1102

JOB OBJECTIVE

A position as a home economist testing new products for a small- to middle-sized firm.

PERSONAL

Will relocate.
Will travel.

WORK HISTORY

1970-1979   Teacher, food chemistry and general home economics, Arlington High School, Kent City, Virginia.

Freelance consultant to three major food firms. Specialized in testing new food products and writing reports suggesting how they might best be marketed.

EDUCATION

1969   Awarded B.S. in home economics. Major: food chemistry. Minor: business administration.

LANGUAGES

1968   Lived and worked in Grenoble, France. Fluent in French. Wrote paper on "Convenience Foods Acceptance in the French Marketplace," accepted for publication in <u>Food Chemistry Journal</u>.

References will be furnished on request.

Dietitian, nutritionist, teacher

HOSPITAL ADMINISTRATOR

James Bell
1300 Avenue A
Temple, Texas 76501
Phone: 444-8090

OBJECTIVE
Responsible middle-management position in major urban hospital. I am especially qualified in the area of purchasing and general operations.

CAPSULE
Have worked for fifteen years in all phases of hospital administration and have developed special expertise in cost cutting while maintaining quality.

EXPERIENCE
<u>Assistant department head buyer, purchasing.</u> Assumed variety of responsibilities in all areas of hospital administration. Gathered information and wrote annual budget-planning report.

<u>Department assistant, Ladywood Hospital.</u> Worked primarily in budgeting and operations. Reduced amounts expended in various supply areas as follows:

Linens	12%
Utilities	3%
Laboratory supplies	20%

EMPLOYMENT HISTORY
1970-present. Mountainside Hospital, Cloverdale, California.

1970-1963. Ladywood Hospital, Boxton, California.

PUBLICATIONS
Report to AMA titled "Hospital Standards Throughout the United States."
HEW report: "Hospital Operations and Middle Management."

PERSONAL
Married.
Will relocate.
Will travel.

EDUCATION
M.A., 1962, public health, University of Michigan.
B.A., 1960, public health and business, Stanford.

REFERENCES
Furnished on request.

Executive, hotel manager, purchasing agent

INDUSTRIAL ENGINEER

INDUSTRIAL ENGINEER

James Teal
303 Austin Drive
Tulsa, Oklahoma   74101
282-0810

Capsule: Seven years experience as industrial engineer specializing in
financial planning and personnel management. Recently passed the exami-
nation for state license. Am seeking position with small industrial firm
where I can be assured of multiple responsibilities and growth.

Work Chronology: 1975 to present. A.B. Johnston, Inc.
Title: senior industrial engineer. Headed team of eight specializing in
financial planning for the firm, which showed a regular annual profit of
$10 million. By cutting costs in supplies and personnel, we were able
to save the company $1.5 million last year. Part of the year was devoted
to an extensive analysis of new products and directions that would be open
to the company in the 1980s.

1972 to 1975. Stonecraft Engineering Industries, Inc.
Began as junior engineer working under supervision of department head.
In 1973, was appointed assistant to department head. In 1974, when department head retired, was appointed to replace him. I introduced the
team study approach, which is still used at the company today.

Education: B.S., engineering, M.I.T., 1972
Full-scholarship student; also worked 30 hours a week for four years
during school.

Personal: Married, with three children
Will travel

References: Furnished on request

Chemical engineer, civil engineer,
electrical engineer, production
manager

INTERIOR DECORATOR

RICHARD SAGE

INTERIOR DESIGNER

66 Park Row   Home: 212-348-9613
New York, New York 10017   Office: 212-440-3201

EMPLOYMENT

1970-1979. Sage Antique Exports, Inc., Paris, France.
Owned antique importing business, dealing mostly with 18th- and
19-century furniture. Also imported some fabric. Recently
sold business because of desire to return to U.S.

1961-1970. Fabric designer, Carlton Furniture Co., New York
City. Designed and produced upholstery fabric.

PROFESSIONAL MEMBERSHIPS

American Society of Interior Designers, since 1969.

EDUCATION

B.A., Rhode Island School of Design, interior design and fabric
design.

PERSONAL

Born 4-13-35
U.S. citizen

Business references available on request.

Department-store manager,
furniture salesperson

JEWELER

<u>Andrew Marley</u>

600 West Ninety-ninth Street   212/666-3890
New York, New York   10025

Job Objective

Seeking management responsibilities in small jewelry store with option
to buy.

Employment

1973 to present. Ring repairer and jewelry salesman.
     Radnor Downtown Jewelers, New York City.

1972-1973. Apprentice modelmaker and stonesetter.
     Chilton Jewelry Manufacturing, New York City.

1968-1971. Apprentice program in colored stone setting.
     Excel Jewelry Manufacturers, New York City.

Education

1964-1968. Radnor High School, Radnor, Pennsylvania.

Personal

Married, with three children
Wish to relocate near but outside New York City
Health excellent
Born 1-20-50

References will be furnished on request.

LABOR-RELATIONS NEGOTIATOR

Stanley James

JOB OBJECTIVE

Position with private industry as labor-negotiator.

CAPSULE HISTORY

Nine years experience with local and state government. Specialties include handling of worker grievances, wage-hour compliance, and contract negotiation.

PERSONAL

1300 West Orange Avenue
West Orange, New Jersey 07052
Phones: 555-0987 (home)
         666-3991 (office)
Will relocate; will travel
Married, with two children

WORK HISTORY

New Jersey Wage and Hour Compliance Agency.
My responsibilities included overseeing union-management relations; investigating wage-and-hour complaints; writing reports recommending action on investigation. A large portion of my time with the agency was spent preparing a 450-page report on the status of the state's affirmative-action programs for the Department of Health, Education, and Welfare.

West Orange City Government, Mayor's Labor Relations Office.
Major areas of responsibility and interest included contract negotiations for city workers, union-management relations, daily labor-relations responsibilities, and handling workers' grievances.

CHRONOLOGY

7-16-73 to present.
New Jersey Wage and Hour Compliance Agency

8-1-63 to 7-13-73.
West Orange City Government, Mayor's Labor-Relations Office.

EDUCATION

M.A., industrial relations, Atlanta State College
B.A., political science, U.C.L.A., with honors
Scholarship student

REFERENCES

Furnished on request

*Attorney, minority-rights worker,
wage and salary administrator*

LABORATORY TECHNICIAN

Barbara Roth
70999 Mercy Lane
Dubuque, Iowa 52001
Phone: 888-7054

Summary: Nine years of experience, five as an assistant laboratory technician working on measles vaccine, and three years as a technician working on
a cancer research project. Have attended various training programs and
seminars in the U.S. and Europe; have presented five papers at seminars.

Objective: Seeking position as senior technician in cancer research.

Employment: Honore Laboratories, Inc., Chicago, Illinois. September 1970-
October 1975. Assistant laboratory technician. Honore, a major drug-
research firm, runs a six-month training program for all new technicians,
in which I was a participant. Was then assigned as assistant laboratory
technician, working under John Gedding, Ph.D., specialist in vaccine research. Worked on long-term vaccine development.

Chem-Ease Laboratories, Dubuque, Iowa. November 1975-present. Laboratory
technician working on cancer research project under supervision of Marya
Knightley, Ph.D. Was sent as company representative to four international
conferences; presented papers on our cancer project at 1977 and 1978 conferences. Three other papers were presented through my initiative at U.S.
Laboratory Technicians for Cancer Research annual meetings.

Education: Purdue University, Ph.D., 1970, oncological research; M.A.,
1964, chemistry; B.A., 1962, chemistry.

*Bacteriologist, biochemist, biologist,
medical technician*

LIBRARIAN

RESUME

Personal

Karl Rozin
422 Martin Street
Stanford, California 94305
Phone: 588-9080

Education

M.A., 1969, U.C.L.A., library science with specialty in acquisitions.
B.A., 1967, San Jose State University, library science.

Languages

Fluent in Spanish; reading knowledge of French and German.

Work Experience

April 1970-present
Assistant librarian, children's department, San Francisco City Library.
Hired to do acquisitions part-time and to develop a summer reading program
for school-age children. Promoted to full librarian, children's department,
June 1976. Supervised a staff of five assistants and did most of the ac-
quisitions work for the children's department.

June 1967-April 1970
General library trainee, San Jose Community Library.
Because library was small, I was able to work in all departments at various
times during my first two years there. In 1969, I was promoted to assistant
children's librarian. Worked to establish interlibrary loan for children's
books. This service has enabled three intercounty libraries to reduce their
acquisitions expenditures by sharing purchases.

Throughout college, I worked as a library assistant in the main university
library.

References

Available on request.

*Corporate librarian, school librarian,
supervisor*

54

MANUFACTURING EXECUTIVE

Benjamin Drew
1821 Maple Heights Drive
Wyckoff, New Jersey 07481
Phone: 202-348-0040

OBJECTIVE	A responsible position offering career opportunity, expansion of knowledge, and an immediate challenge. I am particularly qualified to contribute as a general manager or vice president of manufacturing.
GENERAL	Have held a variety of positions, from foreman to engineer, and am currently totally responsible for the manufacturing management and profitability of a three-facility division of a Fortune 500 firm.

AREAS OF
EXPERIENCE

PRESENT

Manufacturing Manager: Report to the president; have complete responsibility for three manufacturing plants; approximately $30,000,000 sales; 550 employees.

My first four years in this position produced these gains:

Return on assets	increased	570%
Net earnings	increased	450%
Sales	increased	140%

Significant accomplishments:

Scrap	reduced	15%
Productivity	increased	15%
Shipping expense	reduced	25%
Customer returns	reduced	50%
Compensation claims	reduced	50%
Customer service	reduced delivery slips	80%

The above achievements were due to my expertise in analysis; my securing cooperation, competitiveness, and motivation from all concerned and especially between plants; my setting goals with proper and meaningful measurements; and, most of all, my simultaneous involvement in all areas.

I designed and installed our individual facility machine loading-scheduling system, which increases machine utilization and presents backlog vs. capacity, labor needs vs. payroll, and production slip notification.

I negotiated two multiyear union contracts with annual increases under 6% at our New Jersey plant. (Southern plants are non-union.)

Business executive, comptroller, financial analyst, production supervisor, purchasing manager

(Continued)

PRIOR
EXPERIENCE

Systems Engineer: I established the manufacturing standards in all departments in conjunction with the design and implementation of the standard cost system.

Manager of Information Services: I improved and computerized the inventory-control system (Burroughs 342). I also re-designed and converted the sales analysis and the gross profit systems to the parent corporation's central computer (Burroughs 3500).

Product Engineer: My adeptness at analyzing and solving problems quickly resulted in Qualified Product Listings for all military specifications within our manufacturing capabilities. These included Mil-C-17, Mil-C-915, Mil-W-2194, and Mil-W-16878, and required both in-depth knowledge of the characteristics of all available insulating and jacketing materials and the ability to influence cognizant Government officials. Because of my broad product knowledge, I was called into all wire and cable problem areas. I received a commendation from REA (Rural Electrification Agency), together with its approval of my version of our company telephone cable specifications.

Product Manager: I secured complete cooperation and team effort through my ability to anticipate and provide for the total needs of the manufacturing operation. My internal specifications always include step-by-step detail, such as type, size, and number of fillers to fit into cable interstices; picks/inch on a particular type braiding machine; reel type and size as dictated by the operation; in-process and final test requirements and certifications; packing and shipping instructions, etc. Accurate cost-accounting base, correct delivery dates, and precise purchasing information are additional benefits of the complete manufacturing process sheet.

Sales Engineer. I utilized my analytical and engineering abilities to coordinate plant capabilities with customer requirements. I designed the first wires insulated with "Kapton H Film" (Polyimide) for the Titan missile, and co-authored a technical paper on these constructions. I also fashioned the first gas-tight, shielded, silicone rubber cable for the Con Edison nuclear power station.

(Continued)

Foreman (college, senior year): I supervised the magnet
wire department, comprised of 60 men. Improved employee
morale led to fewer union grievances and increased production. This was instrumental in the reinstating of monthly
supervisory bonuses.

EMPLOYMENT   4/1968-present   company name by request--engaged in the
HISTORY   manufacture of bare and plated electrical conductors.

                 2/1967-3/1968   Production Manager, Monolith, Inc.

                 4/1962-1/1967   Product Control Manager, Bable Industries,
Inc.

                 5/1956-3/1962   Cable Engineer, Xenia Products, Inc.

                 2/1954-2/1956   Acting First Sergeant, Xenia Products, Inc.

                 1953   Foreman, Xenia Products, Inc.

PERSONAL   Born May 9, 1931, married, two children, excellent health.
Enjoy tennis, handball, and bowling. Travel extensively
and am willing to relocate.

EDUCATION   Iowa State University, B.S. Industrial Management, 1954
Pace College, Graduate School, 33 credits toward accounting
  M.B.A.
U.S. Army basic electronics and advanced radar schools.

ORGANIZATIONS   American Society for Testing and Materials
National Electrical Manufacturers Association
Society of Automotive Engineers, (A-2H)
  Electrical Wire and Cable Subcommittee

MARKET RESEARCHER

MARKET RESEARCHER

Mindy Pickette
Apartment 2A
Hillside Apartment Complex
Bethesda, Maryland 20014
Phones: 833-8578 (office)
574-1139 (home)

JOB OBJECTIVE

Position as market researcher in food industry, senior analyst level pre-
ferred with supervisory responsibilities.

EMPLOYMENT RECORD

Senior market research analyst, 1971-present
     Chem Food Products, Inc. Responsible for testing and development
     of five new product lines. Devised several approaches for testing,
     did preliminary tests, and wrote recommendations for methods to be
     used in mass market tests.

Research assistant, 1968-1971
     Cornell University, food research department. Responsible for edit-
     ing and coding consumer responses, tabulating survey returns, and
     reporting on consumer survey findings.

EDUCATION

B.S., marketing, 1967; M.A., business administration, Cornell University,
1968

*Home economist, marketing
manager, marketing sales director,
media analyst, nutritionist,
production manager, statistician*

OFFICE MANAGER

Ann N. Wolf
3520 N. Lake Shore Drive
Chicago, Illinois 60657
312-996-2801

JOB RECORD:

July 1968 - present
PGM, Inc., 640 North LaSalle Street, Chicago (337-7676)
Advertising and sales promotion
Office Manager - Bookkeeper
  Supervised a staff of three.
  Handled corporation books, including payroll, accounts payable and
    receivable, billing.
  Shorthand and typing (IBM Executive).
  Proofread copy for ads, catalogues, sales-promotion pieces.
  Handled group health and life insurance and all other company insurance.
  Heavy telephone and in-person contact with clients and suppliers.
  Composed correspondence.
  Acted as administrative assistant to three corporate officers.

April 1965 - July 1968
Hartwig Exhibitions (no longer in business in Chicago)
Designers and manufacturers of trade-show exhibits
Secretary-Receptionist
  Handled reception and phone.
  Took dictation from four salesmen and production manager.
  Typed on IBM Selectric.
  Handled all phases of office work usually associated with a one-girl
    office.

October 1959 - April 1965
Associated Employers of Illinois, 221 North LaSalle Street, Chicago
Non-profit employers' association
Secretary-Receptionist
  Managed one-girl office.
  Transcribed correspondence from shorthand and dictaphone.
  Acted as receptionist and handled phones.
  Did light bookkeeping, including handling membership dues and payroll.
  Planned luncheon and dinner meetings for association members. This
  included handling seating arrangements and coordination with hotels
  where meetings were held.

Business-machine operator, clerk,
executive secretary, public
administrator, stenographer
(Continued)

Previous jobs included four years as secretary to a sales manager of Nu Tone, Inc. (no longer located in Chicago). Took heavy shorthand and also dictaphone. One year with U.S. Army Corps of Engineers as secretary to colonel in charge of supply and procurement division.

EDUCATION:

Foreman High School - general and business courses, graduated.
Wright Junior College - business and fine arts courses, associate degree.
Art Institute of Chicago - one year.

Personal references will be supplied if requested.

PARALEGAL

Susan Goldman   Phone: 212-688-7359

Job Objective: Position with full-time paralegal responsibilities in large law firm in New York area.

Work experience:

1977 to present, secretary-paralegal for Dixon & Dixon, New
York. My position, which began as secretary, has gradually
become full-time paralegal. I spend approximately three days
a week in court, and am familiar with the local, state, and
federal court system.

Education:

1977 to present, attending New York University Law School,
evening division.

1972-1976, New York University. B.A., political science.

Personal:

Reside at 340 West Twenty-third Street
New York, New York 10002

References available on request.

*Legal secretary, court reporter,
office assistant*

PERSONNEL EXECUTIVE

Ruth Ebstein

1800 Terrace Row   Home: 888-0912
Baltimore, Maryland 21200

OBJECTIVE: Key personnel position with a progressive and innovative
               organization.

SUMMARY: Innovative personnel executive with in-depth knowledge of
               the profession. Proficient in organization and manpower
               planning, executive recruiting, wage and salary adminis-
               tration, EEO/Affirmative Action, benefit and pension
               administration, ERISA compliance, program development,
               employee and labor relations, operating and fringe-benefit
               budgeting.

EXPERIENCE: Established personnel department and developed it into a
               contributing force in management operations.

Personnel
Management   Conducted organization analysis and structure, manpower
               planning and development to provide the corporation with
               efficient human resources.

               Increased productivity of professional employees by develop-
               ing and administering extensive and ongoing management-by-
               objectives program.

               Maintained uninterrupted operations, sustaining trained
               manpower during several plant and office relocations.

               Developed preventive medical program to ensure the health
               and safety of employees. Minimized lost time and reduced
               insurance premiums.

Recruitment   Reduced employment costs, accomplished more timely place-
               ments, and improved caliber of new personnel.

               Heavy direct search and selection of managerial, profession-
               al, and technical personnel.

               Established and maintained effective college recruitment
               program.

*Customer relations employment
counselor, minority-rights worker,
wage and salary administrator*   (Continued)

Wage and Salary	Implemented and directed wage and salary programs. (Hay and factor comparison.)
	Improved and maintained incentive and indirect compensation plans.
Government Relations	Reduced exposure to compliance reviews, individual and class-action suits by designing, directing, and implementing EEO/Affirmative Action plans.
	Ensured compliance with the regulatory agencies and labor laws, keeping all levels of management aware of corporate and individual responsibilities.
Benefits	Managed corporate benefit program covering pensions, insured benefits, and company-sponsored programs.
Communications	Contributed to employee understanding of company's business objectives, functions, policies, and guidelines through direction of employee communication and publication program.
Labor and Employee Relations	Strengthened non-union environment by organizing effective labor and employee-relations program in highly organized industry.
	Developed and implemented numerous support programs and policies in communications, management awareness, supervisory training, labor negotiations, employee relations, health and safety.
Training and Development	Enhanced efficiency by improving supervisor/employee rapport through the development of training programs and operating procedures.
	Identified training and development needs of individuals and groups and implemented programs to meet those needs.
	Conducted in-house management seminars to provide knowledge and understanding over a broad spectrum of subjects.
EDUCATION:	B.S., Indiana University, Psychology/Economics, 1955 Numerous business courses at various organizations and institutions.

(Continued)

AFFILIATIONS: Eldorado, Inc.   Director of Personnel
                2/1974-present

                Air Transport Industries   Director of Personnel
                12/71-2/74
                9/59-12/71   Corporate Personnel
                                                   Manager, Director of
                                                   Wage and Salary

PERSONAL: Married, four children
                Will travel/relocate

PROFESSIONAL   American Association of Personnel Administrators
ASSOCIATIONS: New York Personnel Managers Association
                Northern New Jersey Employers Association
                American Compensation Society
                Board of Directors, New Jersey Industrial
                Nurses Association

PHARMACIST

R E S U M E

O F

SOLOMON DIDIER   REGISTERED PHARMACIST
1300 Drivers Lane   Married
Oak Point, Michigan 48237   Will relocate
857-1126 (home)   396-1000 (office)

Objective: Assistant manager's position with large drugstore chain.

Work   1974-present, assistant night manager, Total Drugstores, Inc.
Experience: Supervise three registered pharmacists in this all-night
                drugstore; fill prescriptions, monitor and reorder supplies,
                and supervise point-of-purchase advertising for three major
                display counters.

                1972-1974, pharmaceutical salesperson. Orgon Pharmaceutical
                Supplies, Inc., Indianapolis, Indiana. Covered Indiana,
                Ohio, and northern Michigan. Did some test marketing of new
                product lines in northern Indiana; this entailed introducing
                productions to potential customers and writing reports indi-
                cating their responses.

Education: Master's of Pharmacy, Southern Indiana State University,
                1972. Magna cum laude. (Bachelors and masters program were
                combined into one five-year curriculum.)

Professional   Licensed to practice pharmacy in Illinois, Indiana, and
Information: Ohio.

References: Will be pleased to furnish on request.

Biochemist, technical salesperson

PHOTOGRAPHER'S STYLIST

PHOTOGRAPHY STYLIST

Anne Porter
134 West Ninety-second
New York, New York 10025
Phone: 212-497-2000

GOAL

To work for innovative, active photographer who can and is willing to use
my varied talents.

CAPSULE EXPERIENCE

I have worked as a stylist for five years. Tasks have ranged from locating
an extremely rare antique and negotiating its rental to sewing costumes and
building room-size sets for use as photo props. I have functioned as office
manager and purchasing agent in addition to stylist and would be willing to
handle these responsibilities again.

WORK CHRONOLOGY

October 1974 to present. Chief stylist and office manager for Taber Greene,
photographer specializing in interior and product shots. Supervised secretary, bookkeeper, and receptionist, while assuming major responsibility for
all styling. When necessary, I hired additional persons to help with set
and prop preparation and supervised their work.

August 1973-October 1974. Window dresser, Mann Department Store.

June 1971-August 1973. Girl Friday for fashion photographer. Booked and
helped select models, bought photography supplies, and kept books for
business in addition to secretarial responsibilities.

EDUCATION

B.A., fine arts, Georgia State University, January 1971.

LANGUAGES
Fluent in French.

INTERESTS
Travel, art, reading.

REFERENCES
Furnished on request.

*Photographer, photographer's
assistant, set designer*

PHYSICAL THERAPIST

BETH ANN NELSON

JOB OBJECTIVE

Position as physical therapist that allows a lot of patient contact, preferably with children. Interested in planning and developing physical-therapy programs in addition to administering them.

PERSONAL

Single; excellent health; will relocate; will travel
Reside at 15 Country Club Plaza, Kansas City, Kansas 64108
Phone: 317-350-1042, Extension 330.

PROFESSIONAL

Licensed to practice physical therapy by State of Kansas.

EMPLOYMENT

1974-1979, physical therapist, Dwayne Hospital.
Perform and interpret diagnostic tests and write programs for individual therapy, which are then carried out by staff therapist. Check after six and twelve weeks to make any needed adjustments in programs.

1973-1974, physical therapist, Rehabilitation Center.
Worked part-time while attending school. Assisted therapists with swimming therapy.

EDUCATION

B.A., physical therapy, January 1974, Utah Western University.
B.A., physical education, June 1973, Utah Western University.
Have completed nine hours toward master's in physical therapy.

References on request.

*Occupational therapist, nurse,
paramedic*

PLANT MANAGER

Resume of

Ralph Brunton

122 Western Street

Detroit, Michigan 48200

Phone: 344-0900

Job Objective

Plant manager in medium to large manufacturing company.

Work Experience

1960-Present, ABC Manufacturing Parts Company. Hired as assistant to
plant manager on night shift, where I worked for three years. Promoted
to assistant to plant manager on day shift in 1972. Became plant manager in 1973. Reorganized work schedules to permit 4 1/2-day work week
at same level of productivity and introduced swing shift as an option
for workers who desired it.

1955-1960, DEF Motor Company. Assembly-line worker. Served as union
representative for three years.

Education

1958-1960. Attended junior college, taking accounting and business-math
courses.

1958, graduated from Lane Vocational High School, Detroit, Michigan.

Special Achievements

As union representative, I assisted in contract negotiations on three
occasions. As company representative, I attended a seminar on plant
managers and labor relations organized by the U.S. Department of Labor.
I have developed a specialty in labor relations that I feel would contribute to my ability to run a plant efficiently.

*Foreman, mailroom supervisor,
production manager, supervisor*

PRODUCT MANAGER

<u>Roberta Wells</u>

1300 Wilson Avenue
St. Louis, Missouri   63119
Phone: 487-4855

<u>Job Objective</u>

Position as designer of women's apparel

<u>Employment History</u>

Junior House Designs, Ltd., 1976-1979

    <u>Trainee</u>. Worked as a sample maker, pattern maker, cutter, and machine operator.

    <u>Assistant product manager</u>. Responsibilities included estimating production costs, scheduling work flow, hiring and training new workers, controlling quality, supervising overall production activities, some bookkeeping.

<u>Education</u>

Rhode Island School of Design, 1972-1976

    Scholarship student
    Awarded Golden Ace Student Design Award
    Design, major; business administration, minor

<u>Personal</u>

Married, with one child
Will relocate; will travel

References and samples available on request.

Buyer, clothes designer, fashion coordinator, inventory-control administrator, production supervisor, purchasing agent

PROFESSIONAL HOUSEKEEPER

Paula Birnbaum   Single
1822 Tinkers Row   No children
Columbus, Ohio   44020   Will travel
Phone: 399-0010   Will relocate

JOB TITLE

Professional housekeeper

EMPLOYMENT RECORD

January 1976-   Assistant Buyer, paper and linen supplies.
present   Bedside Inn Motels, Inc. Sunnybrook Vale, Idaho.
                 Assisted in buying paper supplies for thirty hotels
                 in five-state area. Arranged delivery times and
                 coordinated deliveries. Promoted to department
                 buyer for linens.

August 1973-   Assistant housekeeper, XYZ Hotel, Los Angeles,
January 1976   California. Originally supervised staff of twenty
                 who bought linen and paper supplies. Promoted to
                 buyer for kitchen supplies. Supervised buying staff
                 of twenty-three. XYZ is a 350-room hotel geared
                 mostly to convention and summer-vacation business.

EDUCATION AND PROFESSIONAL HONORS

Certified member of National Executive Housekeeping Association.

Graduate, Oakdale High School, Los Angeles, California, top third of
class, 1973.

Have taken the following courses in night school:

 Business math I and II
 Hotel management I-IV

Inventory-control administrator,
purchasing agent

PSYCHIATRIC NURSE

Madeleine Taylor

PERSONAL

Date of Birth:	May 27, 1951
Place of Birth:	Chicago, Illinois
Correspondence Address:	Apt. 2002 4343 North Clarendon Avenue Chicago, Illinois 60613
Phone:	(312) 281-6296 Home (312) 975-5101 Work
License Number:	41-141739

EDUCATION

May 1979	M.S.N., St. Xavier College, Chicago, Illinois
August 1976	B.S.N., University of Rhode Island
June 1972	Diploma, Michael Reese Hospital and Medical Center School of Nursing, Chicago, Illinois

PROFESSIONAL BACKGROUND

1978-79	Clinical Internship; intakes, supervised individual, marital, family, and group psychotherapy	Community Mental Health Clinic St. Joseph Hospital Chicago, Illinois
1978	Clinical Internship; intakes, supervised individual and family psychotherapy	Mental Health Clinic Grant Hospital Chicago, Illinois
1976-present	Clinical Nursing Instructor and Coordinator, Nursing I; clinical and classroom instruction. Coordinator, Nursing II (psychiatric nursing).	Augustana Hospital School of Nursing Chicago, Illinois
1975-76	Psychiatric Nurse Clinician; evaluation of outpatients with emotional problems, supervision of individual psychotherapy and patient management, psychiatric consultation to medical-surgical units	Mental Health Clinic Day-Kimball Hospital Putnam, Connecticut

Hospital administrator, nurse, psychologist, social worker

(Continued)

1975	Staff Nurse in alcoholic treatment center; care of the alcoholic during the initial drying-out period and involvement in rehabilitation	Starlight Farms, Inc. Stonington, Connecticut
1974	Assistant Head Nurse; supervision and administration, in-service education, and individual therapy	Illinois State Psychiatric Institute, Chicago, Illinois
1972-74	Staff Nurse; milieu therapy, group therapy, and patient-care planning and treatment	Illinois State Psychiatric Institute Chicago, Illinois
1972	Staff Nurse; primary nursing care on a cardio-vascular thoracic surgical unit	University of Chicago Hospitals and Clinics Chicago, Illinois

PAPERS AND PUBLICATIONS

"The Nurse as a Psychotherapist," submitted for publication to Psychotherapy: Theory, Research and Practice.
"The Nurse as a Psychiatric Consultant." In preparation.

PUBLIC RELATIONS EXECUTIVE

Judith Golden
1600 Main Street
Wilmington, New York 12997
Phone: 860-3123

PERSONAL

Single
Will travel
Will relocate

OBJECTIVE

Managerial position with major corporation in public relations department; would prefer to work with products rather than services.

EMPLOYMENT
7/74-
present

Vice president, Allied Public Relations, Ltd. Supervise staff of three writers. Work with suppliers to buy graphic arts outside firm. Major responsibilities include planning annual public relations activities for five clients, whose products range from tissue paper to school supplies to collectors' plates.

4/72-
7/74

Account executive. Responsibilities were basically the same; I brought the five aforementioned clients to the firm.

1/69-
4/72

Executive secretary to president. Besides regular responsibilities, I started and was responsible for an internal employees' newsletter, which is still being published.

4/68-
1/69

Volunteer director, New Careers for Divorced Women. In addition to handling overall administrative responsibilities, I supervised a volunteer staff of twenty part-timers. A major part of my time was spent organizing and assigning projects and checking to make sure they were completed by the target date. Close supervision was necessitated by the restrictions of working with a part-time staff. Wrote grant proposals that brought our organization $450,000 in federal and state monies, an increase of $300,000 over previous years. Wrote and did production work on series of twenty booklets designed to show divorced women how to re-enter the job market.

EDUCATION

B.S., home economics, Oregon State University, 1954, graduated with honors. Class standing: 2 out of 350.

REFERENCES

Will be furnished on request.

House-organ editor, management consultant, media director, media trainee, press agent

PURCHASING AGENT

SAM NUSBAUM

PURCHASING AGENT

430 Liberty Drive
Apartment 1900
Boston, Massachusetts 02151
Phone: 857-9375

WORK HISTORY

<u>Assistant Buyer</u>   <u>1975-present</u>
M & N Engineering Corporation, Boston, Massachusetts
Responsible for buying technical-division supplies; budget allowed is
$4 million annually.

<u>Junior purchasing agent</u>   <u>1971-1975</u>
Technical Supplies, Inc., Boston, Massachusetts
Began with very comprehensive training program that included three months
in storekeeper's section and three months in buying. After four-month
trial period in buying, assumed responsibility for buying standard office
supplies. In 1974, was promoted to assistant buyer for laboratory supplies
and given responsibility for a $2 million budget.

EDUCATION

M.A., Indiana University, business, 1971
B.A., Purdue University, business management and computer science, 1970
Have attended seminars and taken two post-graduate courses in purchasing
to increase expertise in my field.

PROFESSIONAL HONORS

Applied for Certified Purchasing Manager, awarded by National Association
of Purchasing Management; approval pending, expected in spring 1979.

*Management trainee, purchasing
manager, sales promoter*

74

REAL ESTATE BROKER

REAL ESTATE BROKER

Janet Jayson

589 Indigo Drive
West Lafayette, Indiana 47906
Phone: 317-857-9486

Experience

1975-present

Aaron Realty, Inc. During the years I have
worked for this company, I have generated
$3 million in home sales. In 1978, I was
named "Best Realtor" for a five-state region.
I am licensed by the State of Indiana.

Education

1950-1954

Round Hill Teachers' College, Round Hill,
North Carolina. B.A., elementary education.

Personal

From 1954 until 1975, I reared three children, was active in
many community organizations and substituted in the elementary
school system approximately 100 days per year. My children
are now college age, and I am looking for full-time, permanent
employment.

Willing to travel. References on request.

*Real estate sales manager, real
estate salesperson, returning
housewife*

RECEPTIONIST

Georgina Martin

190 Austin Drive
Apartment 313
Shawnee Mission, Kansas 66205
Phone: 384-4817

Employment

August 1977-present

Part-time receptionist for
Rollins Textbook Publishers.

January 1975-August 1977

Full-time receptionist for
Edison, Inc., manufacturing firm
with 220 employees. Filled in
on CENTREX switchboard.

Education

1977-present

Part-time student at Trenton
Community College, working on
B.A. in business administration.

References available.

*General office worker, hospital
receptionist, stenographer, typist*

RESTAURANT MANAGER

JOHN ANDERSON

1700 Oneida Drive   Monterey, California 93940
499-1944 (office)   456-1134 (home)

WORK EXPERIENCE

<u>Assistant restaurant manager</u>, Skyline Grill, Skyline City, California.
May 1973 to present. This restaurant is known for the elegance of its
table settings and food presentation, as well as the excellence of its
kitchen. My responsibilities include working closely with the head chef,
ordering food and planning menus, supervising a staff of fifty-five,
ordering all supplies, general budgeting, and maintaining payroll records.

<u>Assistant restaurant manager and host</u>, ABC Restaurants, Inc., Norfolk,
Virginia. May 1971-May 1973.

<u>Short-order chef</u>, ABC Restaurants, Inc., at main store, located in
Louisville, Kentucky. January 1973-May 1973.

EDUCATION

Dexter Junior College, Dexter, Kentucky, awarded associate degree in
restaurant management, June 1973.

Dexter High School, Dexter, Kentucky, graduated January 1971.

PERSONAL

Married; will relocate.

*Chef, food-services worker, hotel
manager, purchasing agent,
purchasing manager*

RETAIL CLOTHING BUYER

Stephen Lieberman
800 Central Park West, Apt. 12
New York, New York 10022
948-9487 (evenings)
857-9487 (daytime)

Summary

Six years' experience in retail clothing, specializing in women's wear.
Committed to field and seeking position that offers greater responsibility,
more challenge, and room for growth.

Employment History

Buyer, Mini-sette Clothes, Inc., 1974-present
Supervision of sales staff of fifteen; checking invoices of materials
received; working with point-of-sale computer terminals to keep up-to-the-
minute sales records; writing quarterly report evaluating sales and
projecting sales for next quarter.

Buyer Trainee, Juniorettes, Inc., 1972-1974
Worked one month each in sales, stock, reorder, and bookkeeping. After
training, I worked as a salesperson while assisting with buying. Responsible for coordinating the fall and spring sales catalogues; worked closely
with copywriters and art department.

Education

B.A., Boston State University School of Design, business marketing, 1972.
Curriculum included a three-month internship in local department store;
afterward I worked in the store as part-time sales help.

Graduated from Boston Central High School, 1968.

Personal

Will travel; will relocate.

References

Available on request.

*Buyer trainee, department store
manager, estimator, manufacturer's
representative, retail-store
manager, sales promoter, wholesale
clothing buyer*

RETAIL FOOD BUYER

RESUME OF

REBECCA SWAIN

1400 Round Hill Drive   Phone: 398-2464
Indianapolis, Indiana   46200

Job Objective:

Challenging position in food management with growth-oriented company.

Work History:

Assistant store manager, Roberts Groceries, Inc.
March 1977 to present
Responsibilities included working in all phases of store management and
coordinating store activities; on several occasions, I filled in for
store manager for two-week periods. Supervised staff of fifty-five.

Salesperson, ABC Canned Foods Supplies, Inc.
September 1975 to February 1977
Traveled in three-state area selling canned foods products lines to
grocery stores. Increased business overall by 250 percent, and picked
up approximately twenty new customers.

Store management trainee, Roberts Groceries, Inc.
July 1974 to September 1975
Six-month training program introduced me to all facets of in-store food
management as well as warehousing, transportation, and accounting. After
training program, I worked in purchasing for six months.

Education:

B.S., Cornell University; major, food management; minor, computer science

Have taken Cornell home-study courses in food distribution, security, and
    food transportation.

*Estimator, food-services worker,
home economist, manufacturer's
representative, purchasing agent,
supermarket manager*

RETAIL SALESPERSON

R E T A I L   S A L E S P E R S O N

John Waverly
1890 Tiverton Lane
Milwaukee, Wisconsin   53207
Phone: 866-0330

OBJECTIVE   Retail furniture buyer

EXPERIENCE

September 1959   Senior furniture buyer for ABC Department Store in
to Present   Milwaukee. Responsible for all buying of upholstered
                   furniture. Traveled four times a year to regional
                   distributor shows and bought in-store from sales-
                   persons who handled our account. Responsible for
                   monitoring stock and reordering.

July 1948   Employed in various capacities in Milwaukee department
to August 1959   store, the Emporium. Began as sales trainee and was
                   gradually assigned to all departments in addition to
                   working exchange counter. In 1950, became a full-
                   time salesperson in housewares. In 1952, became
                   assistant buyer in housewares.

                   In 1955, promoted to salesperson in furniture depart-
                   ment, where I began working on commission. My commis-
                   sions averaged about 20 percent higher than average,
                   and I estimate that my efforts increased sales in
                   department by approximately $80,000 per year.

                   In 1957, became assistant buyer of furniture.

EDUCATION

1954   Awarded associate degree from junior community college

1945   Graduated from Milwaukee Central High School

MILITARY

1945 to 1948   U.S. Navy, intelligence

1948 to 1954   U.S. Navy Reserves

PERSONAL   Married twenty-two years; three children.

Furniture salesperson, retail sales
clerk, retail store manager

SALES REPRESENTATIVE

MICHAEL JAMIESON
1458 North Cleveland
Chicago, Illinois 60640
Phone: 312/858-9201

JOB OBJECTIVE

Position in sales management with innovative textbook company.

WORK HISTORY

Sales representative, Alton Social Science Publisher, 1975 - present.
Covered all Midwest with exception of Chicago. Sold forty-five-book line
that spanned three disciplines. Profits for the territory I covered
increased by the following amounts:

10%, 1975; 28%, 1976; 44%, 1977.

Sales representative, Education Books, Inc., 1974 - 1975.
Responsible for five-state territory in South. Sold thirty books spanning
two disciplines, plus two multimedia kits. Profits in my territory jumped
28% over previous year.

EDUCATION

Boston University, 1974
B.A., English literature and business administration

PERSONAL

Birth date: 7-20-56

Health: Excellent

Willing to relocate

Willing to travel

REFERENCES

Furnished on request

*Manufacturer's representative,
publishing trainee, technical
salesperson*

SOCIOLOGIST

JANETTE TRAYNOR

14 Knightbridge Road
Apartment 12
Alexandria, Virginia   22305
Phones: 202-555-9481 (home)
         202-347-1160 (office)

EMPLOYMENT

1972-present   Research analyst, Department of Health, Education, and
                 Welfare. Interpreted statistics for ongoing project
                 on health of school-age children in Appalachia; par-
                 ticipated in writing 600-page summary report. Other
                 projects included analyzing statistics on food value
                 in school lunch, rising cholesterol levels in children
                 under ten, and snack habits of school-age children

1973-1974   Freelance consultant to Tri-Town Family Counseling
                 Center. Did group and individual counseling with
                 emotionally disturbed children.

EDUCATION

1969-1972   Tri-State Southern University, Ph.D., ethnic studies
                 and race relations

1968-1969   Marymount Women's University, M.A., urban sociology

1964-1968   Marymount Women's University, B.A., sociology

PERSONAL

                 Single, with two children
                 Will relocate

REFERENCES

                 On request

*Caseworker, counselor, family
counselor, job guidance counselor,
medical social worker, occupational
therapist, medical social worker,
police officer, psychologist, social
worker*

SPEECH THERAPIST

LOUISE WHEATLEY-SPEECH THERAPIST

PERSONAL
Born 4-11-49
Married, with three children
Health: excellent

487 Round Oak Drive
Providence, Rhode Island 02903
465-7900 (home)

WORK HISTORY

April 1975-
present

Area school therapist. Round Oak County School System.
Primary responsibilities include supervising six other
workers in the three-school area; counseling therapists
as they plan individual therapy for their patients; in-
terpreting test materials for individuals with speech
problems; and routinely testing all first-, third-, and
sixth-graders annually. Develop and conduct group speech
therapy: same age groups of six children work together
for an hour each week. For children who have been pro-
gressing slowly, the results are better than in individual
therapy.

June 1973-
April 1975

Speech rehabilitation therapist. Dixon Rehabilitation
Clinic. Worked with persons suffering from brain damage
and speech impairments that were not birth-related.
Planned and carried out individual therapy.

PROFESSIONAL MEMBERSHIPS AND HONORS

Certified to teach in State of Rhode Island
Certificate of Clinical Competence (Speech)

PUBLICATIONS

"Group Speech Therapy for Grade Schoolers," published May 1977 in
Speech Therapist.
"Group Therapy for Problem Speakers," published August 1977 in Speech
and Hearing Therapist.

EDUCATION

M.A., Purdue University, clinical speech therapy
B.A., Minnesota State University, education and speech pathology
Scholarship student and worked part-time throughout school

*Occupational therapist, psychologist,
sociologist*

83

TEACHER

ELEMENTARY SCHOOL TEACHER

Dorothy Donberg
440 Melrose
Chicago, Illinois 60657
Phone: 312-558-4700

WORK EXPERIENCE

1974-present   Rockport Elementary School, third-grade teacher.

1973   Rockport Elementary School, special-education teacher.
                 Developed program for bilingual students in Spanish.

EDUCATION

1968-1972   Northern Illinois Teachers' College.
                 Graduated magna cum laude.

Present   Have accumulated nine hours for master's in public
                 school administration and expect to complete degree in
                 1980.

EXTRACURRICULAR ACTIVITY

1973   Presented paper, "The Bilingual Child in the Chicago
                 School System," at Chicago Regional Teachers' Con-
                 ference.

PERSONAL

                 Single; will relocate.

References on request.

TECHNICAL WRITER

SUZANNE BECKETT

Goal

Position as technical writer in private sector where I can use my expertise and experience in agricultural research.

Work experience

1970-present. Technical writer, Atlantis Oil Co.
Responsible for all stages of preparation of field-use manuals and fund-request reports. Occasionally write articles for company publication.

1965-1970. Research assistant, Department of Agriculture.
From 1967, also served as associate editor of newsletter directed to oil industry.

Educational background

B.A., agricultural science (major), journalism (minor), Johnson Valley College, 1960

Military service

Served two years in WACS. Stationed in Germany. Honorably discharged with rank of captain. Contributed to Western European U.S. Army newspaper published in Germany, and also worked as technical writer on medical projects.

Skills

Good at organizing and simplifying complex material
Research
Writing
Familiar with computers and their use in research

Personal

2799 Davenport Drive
Tulsa, Oklahoma 74101
Phone: 232-1970

References available on request
Will relocate

*Direct-mail writer, journalist,
reporter, researcher, writer*

TRAVEL AGENT

MARY McCABE - TRAVEL AGENT

JOB OBJECTIVE

Having recently become a certified travel agent in Illinois, I am seeking a position planning international travel with a medium- to large-sized agency.

WORK HISTORY

1975-present   <u>Ticketing agent</u>. Europa Travel Agency, Chicago.

1972-1975   <u>Secretary</u>. Flyaway Travel Agency. After one year, I began to assist agents booking domestic and international flights.

TRAVEL EXPERIENCE

Have traveled to U.S.S.R., Mexico, Western and Eastern Europe--thirty-five countries. Lived in Paris, France, for six months and in Aix-en-Provence for four months.

LANGUAGES

Fluent in French and German

EDUCATION

1971   Graduated, Altamont High School
         Honor Society, cheerleader (three years)

1972   Attended Eastern Women's College, studied French

PERSONAL

500 Michigan Terrace
Chicago, Illinois 60606
Phone: 312/444-0800

References available on request.

Airline reservationist, linguist, reservationist

TYPESETTING SHOP MANAGER

RESUME

Paul Petri

1236 West Eddy Street
Chicago, Illinois 60657
312 472 8352

Birth Date:
January 16, 1946

WORK EXPERIENCE

<u>12/76 to present:</u> Adopt, Inc. <u>Manager, Composition Services.</u> I organized
the art production department, which was formed by a large Chicago commercial printer to provide it with non-union support services. Under my
supervision, this department has grown from a one-person, one-machine
operation to an efficient six-person, two-shift shop. All routines, proto-
cols, and standards for the production of type were instituted by me.

<u>11/74 to 12/76:</u> United Press Midwest (financial printing). <u>Planner/Proof-
reader/Typesetter.</u> Supervised job flow in a twenty-person composing room,
computerized pagination and mark-up of indentures, debentures, and most
other types of legal and financial documents to conform to SEC standards.
Acted as assistant to manager.

<u>9/73 to 11/74:</u> Nurses Association of America. <u>Editorial Assistant and
Writer.</u> I held two positions. First, as an editorial assistant on a
bimonthly medical journal, I was involved with manuscript production,
correspondence, and minute-taking. Second, as an editorial writer for the
Committee on Functions and Standards, I organized, edited, and rewrote the
work of a committee of nursing professionals formed to define the legal
role of OB-GYN-Neonatal nurse practitioners.

<u>10/72 to 8/73:</u> S. Simon Publishing Company. <u>Manuscript Coder.</u> Coded and
typeset copy for the trade and educational divisions.

<u>12/70 to 5/72:</u> Credit Information Corporation of Chicago. <u>Credit Informa-
tion Reporter.</u> On-line terminal operator for computerized credit reporting
system (part time).

<u>9/68 to 9/70:</u> Chicago Speakers Council. <u>Director of Speakers Bureau.</u>
Worked to obtain speakers on a wide range of topics related to U.S. foreign
policy for colleges, clubs, business groups, and educational organizations.

<u>5/68 to 9/68:</u> A.A.A. Corporation (Point Barrow Naval Arctic Research Site).
<u>Administrative Assistant.</u> Duties were directly related to the fulfillment
of documentation standards set by a Government-maintenance contract that
the company held.

*Advertising traffic manager,
management trainee, offset machine
operator, printer, production
manager*

(Continued)

87

EDUCATION

9/65 to 5/67: La Universidad de las Americas (Pueblo, Mexico). Liberal arts curriculum with a major in creative writing. Worked for school administration to meet tuition expenses.

6/64: Graduated from Lyons Township High School, La Grange, Illinois.

SKILLS

Budget management, computerized pagination, editorial, mark-up, paste-up, proofreading, Spanish, supervision, type production. Good supervisory skills.

UNDERWRITER

LINDA FOGARTY

JOB OBJECTIVE   Position as underwriter in small- to middle-size insurance
company. Seeking job that will offer growth to managerial
responsibilities.

WORK   Hilton Insurance Agencies United, Inc.
EXPERIENCE   Underwriter, 1976 to present
Senior claims representative, 1974-1976
My special area of expertise is in major medical policies;
I have a good mastery of medical terminology.

Downing Insurance Company, Inc.
Junior claims representative, 1973-1974
I began in the training program and was advanced to handling
my own claims after six weeks.

Hedrick and Sons, Counselors
Legal secretary, 1972-1973
My work as a legal secretary to three lawyers who specialized
in insurance claims awakened my interest in the insurance
business; it also afforded me an opportunity to become thor-
oughly familiar with the legal terms related to insurance
work.

EDUCATION   B.A., liberal arts, Iowa State University, 1972. Major,
literature; minor, business and management
Graduated from Iowa City High School, 1968

PERSONAL   9487 Shiveley Lane
Elkhart, Indiana 46514
Phone: 948-0397
Will travel, will relocate
Single, good health

*Insurance-claims specialist, wage
and salary administrator*

UNIVERSITY ADMINISTRATOR

RESUME

ALAN GLEN
30 Russian Hill
Apartment 3R
San Francisco, California 94102
Telephone: 280-2843

PROFESSIONAL INTERESTS

Operations and budget management
Research, analysis, and policy determination in higher education.

WORK EXPERIENCE

1972-present: Assistant Vice President, Northern California University
Senior staff officer to Executive Vice President for Administration
Extensive responsibilities in operations management (buildings and grounds,
   administrative services, budget management)
Direct supervision of Office of Publications and Printing
Analyze budget submissions, prepare reports, draft 90% of correspondence
   from office of Executive Vice President
Liaison with purchasing, construction, buildings and grounds, personnel
   management, other support functions
Acting Equal Opportunity and affirmative-action officer (since May 1978)

1967-1972: Assistant Professor of History, University of Southern Michigan
Taught variety of courses in modern European history
Extensive departmental administrative responsibilities, including coordina-
   tion of counseling program

OTHER WORK EXPERIENCE

Sports writer for Dallas Times Herald, text researcher for Screen Gems
   documentary on Truman Administration, speechwriter/researcher in public
   relations firm, copyboy for NBC News

BIOGRAPHICAL DATA

Born December 31, 1940, in Dallas, Texas
Attended public schools in Duncanville (Texas) and Dallas
1958-62, Southern Methodist University (B.A.)
1962-65, Columbia University (M.A., Ph.D.)
Numerous academic honors and awards, including Phi Beta Kappa and
   Woodrow Wilson Fellowship
Fluent in Spanish
Single

*Business executive, principal, public
administrator, school administrator*

URBAN PLANNER

Evan Sims
7400 Lake Shore Drive
Round Lake, Mississippi 39663

555-1100 (office)   456-8827 (home)

CAPSULE

After ten years in publishing and public relations work, I returned to
school for a master's degree in urban planning. It was my intent to combine
my publishing experience with urban planning. Having now worked three years
in urban planning, I am seeking a position that offers the opportunity to
combine my skills with some managerial responsibilities.

WORK HISTORY

1972-present. Editor, Regional Transportation Agency. Supervise staff of
two editors. Responsibilities: information gathering, writing, editing,
and production on twelve annual 48-page reports published by the agency,
in addition to writing and editing the annual budget report.

1968-1970. Assistant editor, social sciences, Martoni Publishing. Edited
fourth-grade social-science text that was part of basal series. Purchased
photography and supervised production of graphics. Worked closely with
authors.

1967-1968. Junior account executive, James International Public Relations
Consultants. Responsibilities: planning marketing campaigns under supervision of senior account executive; writing and production work for these
campaigns.

EDUCATION

1972. Master's degree in urban planning from Round Lake University.
Thesis: "The Role of Publications in Transportation Agencies."

1967. B.A. in liberal arts from Mississippi Southern State University.

REFERENCES

Furnished on request.

*Junior editor, senior editor,
sociologist, technical writer*

4 GETTING READY TO WRITE A RESUME

This is the most important step in resume writing. It is the analytical stage, in which you consider carefully what new directions you can take or how you can put your skills and talents to their best use. It is a time to weed out those responsibilities in which you take little pleasure and to think of ways to emphasize the tasks you truly enjoy. It is also a time to gather enough basic material about yourself so that, by drawing on the information you have so carefully gathered, you are able to write any number of resumes slanted to various job possibilities.

Job hunting is a turning point in your life, regardless of whether or not you are doing it voluntarily, and this is the stage of resume writing where you take into account who you are and where you hope to go.

The first step in the self-analysis—and preparing your resume—is the gathering of facts. Although much of this information may seem too elementary to write down, committing it to paper causes you to think about your accomplishments, as well as your strengths and weaknesses and how they will help or hinder you on any job you accept.

Such self-analysis is not pure self-indulgence. It will help you sort out the kind of job you want and the kind of job you might best avoid, either because you would not be happy doing it or because you would not do it well.

The worksheet that follows combines a mixture of questions: some will uncover basic facts about yourself; others will cause you to think about your job needs, wants, and capacities. Some of the questions in the latter part of the questionnaire will never make it to the final form of your resume. They are important, however, because they will contribute to the tone and attitude of your resume.

Think carefully before you answer these questions. Make your answers as honest as possible. This worksheet is your personal property, and no one else need ever see what you have written.

One suggestion may help you fill in this worksheet: complete the section entitled "Analyzing Your Abilities" and then put it aside for several days. Return to it later, when you bring to it the objectivity of a little distance.

All the information you will supply on these pages could obviously be written on separate sheets of paper; you may even be tempted to do so in order to avoid messing up a book. But this book is intended to function as a workbook. It is meant to be your personal work record. If you gather this material in a permanent place, you will have to go through this stage only once. In the future, updating your resume will simply be a matter of reviewing these forms and updating them.

PERSONAL AND JOB HISTORY WORKSHEET

Section A. Education Information

List exact years of high school attendance._____

What schooling did you have after high school? Check one.

Vocational training_____

Apprenticeship_____

Junior or two-year college_____

College_____ Number of years attended_____

List the dates of your advanced schooling, giving month and year if possible. _____

_____

_____

_____

Write the names and addresses of the schools.

_____

_____

_____

What was your major? _____

What was your minor? _____

94

What subjects did you enjoy most? _____

_____

_____

What subjects did you enjoy least? _____

_____

_____

List any extracurricular activities you were involved in.

_____

_____

_____

What skills or talents did you use in these activities? _____

_____

How might any of these skills or talents have a bearing on any work
you do today or hope to do?

_____

_____

_____

_____

Did you work summers or part-time while attending school?_____
If so, describe the amount of time you spent working and the
responsibilities, skills, and talents you developed through work.

_____

_____

_____

_____

Describe how these responsibilities, skills, and talents might help
you in work you do or hope to do. _____

_____

_____

_____

_____

List six skills or talents that you feel have emerged during your post-
education years.

1. _____

2. _____

3. _____

4. _____

5. _____

6. _____

How might these be applied to work you do or hope to do today?

_____

_____

_____

_____

List and describe any important or major honors received in high school or college (honors society, cum laude or magna cum laude, editorships, presidencies of clubs, etc.). _____

_____

_____

_____

_____

Section B.
Work History

Beginning with your most recent job, list every job you have held full-time, and fill in the information requested on the forms that follow.

Company name: _____

Dates of employment: _____

Brief description of company: _____

_____

Address: _____
                (street)

_____
   (town)   (state)   (zip)

Job title when you began: _____

Job title when you left: _____

Responsibilities and projects undertaken while employed by this company (do not forget to list one-time work assignments as well as daily tasks): _____

_____

_____

_____

_____

_____

_____

What tasks or responsibilities did you most enjoy doing and why?

_____

_____

_____

_____

What tasks or responsibilities did you least enjoy doing and why?

_____

_____

_____

_____

Describe the skills you feel you most developed during this period of employment. _____

_____

_____

_____

_____

Company name: _____

Dates of employment: _____

Brief description of company: _____

_____

Address: _____
            (street)

_____

    (town)   (state)   (zip)

Job title when you began: _____

Job title when you left: _____

Responsibilities and projects undertaken while employed by this company (do not forget to list one-time work assignments as well as daily tasks): _____

_____

_____

_____

_____

_____

_____

What tasks or responsibilities did you most enjoy doing and why?

_____

_____

_____

_____

What tasks or responsibilities did you least enjoy doing and why?

_____

_____

_____

_____

Describe the skills you feel you most developed during this period of employment. _____

_____

_____

_____

_____

Company name: _____

Dates of employment: _____

Brief description of company: _____

_____

Address: _____
                    (street)

_____

   (town)   (state)   (zip)

Job title when you began: _____

Job title when you left: _____

Responsibilities and projects undertaken while employed by this company (do not forget to list one-time work assignments as well as daily tasks): _____

_____

_____

_____

_____

_____

_____

What tasks or responsibilities did you most enjoy doing and why?

_____

_____

_____

_____

What tasks or responsibilities did you least enjoy doing and why?

_____

_____

_____

_____

Describe the skills you feel you most developed during this period
of employment. _____

_____

_____

_____

_____

Company name: _____

Dates of employment: _____

Brief description of company: _____

_____

Address: _____
                        (street)

_____

      (town)   (state)   (zip)

Job title when you began: _____

Job title when you left: _____

Responsibilities and projects undertaken while employed by this
company (do not forget to list one-time work assignments as well as
daily tasks): _____

_____

_____

_____

_____

_____

_____

What tasks or responsibilities did you most enjoy doing and why?

_____

_____

_____

What tasks or responsibilities did you least enjoy doing and why?

_____

_____

_____

Describe the skills you feel you most developed during this period of employment. _____

_____

_____

_____

_____

Company name: _____

Dates of employment: _____

Brief description of company: _____

_____

Address: _____
                    (street)

_____

(town)   (state)   (zip)

Job title when you began: _____

Job title when you left: _____

Responsibilities and projects undertaken while employed by this company (do not forget to list one-time work assignments as well as daily tasks): _____

_____

_____

_____

_____

_____

_____

What tasks or responsibilities did you most enjoy doing and why?

_____

_____

_____

What tasks or responsibilities did you least enjoy doing and why?

_____

_____

_____

Describe the skills you feel you most developed during this period of employment. _____

_____

_____

_____

_____

Using a scale of 1 to 5, with 1 being "not very good" and 5 being "very good to excellent," rate yourself at each skill. Do this as objectively as possible, based on what you know about yourself and what others have told you (in job reviews, for example), because it is to your advantage to weed out the tasks you do not particularly enjoy doing and to discover the kinds of work you truly enjoy. Circle the numbers and put them right above the skills you listed.

Section C. Analyzing Your Abilities

Most of the information you have filled in on these worksheets, such as your job history, education, and personal information, will be rewritten into resume format. The final lists of your strengths and weaknesses may or may not be used in the actual resume. In some occupations, for example, you do list your skills, because they are easily outlined and vital to how well you know your job. In most jobs, though, skills and talents are subtler and less easily pinned down in a word or a short phrase.

Whether or not you use this list directly on your resume, it is a very important part of your job search. You can write a strong resume only if it is very clear in your mind what you want and how you hope to obtain it. Indirectly, the lists that follow will figure in your resume because they will give you a new self-awareness that will enable you to slant your resume not only to your qualifications but to the kind of work you most enjoy doing.

Review all the information you have compiled thus far. Using this information, compile a list of your strongest skills and talents.

1. _____
2. _____
3. _____
4. _____
5. _____

Now compile a list of your weaknesses and the things you least like doing.

1. _____
2. _____
3. _____
4. _____
5. _____

Section D.
Personal Information

Is there anything in your family or personal background—fluency in a language, years lived abroad, book reviews you wrote for your local newspaper—that relates to the job you hope to obtain. If so, describe it below.

_____

_____

Birth date: _____

Are you willing to travel? _____

Are you willing to relocate? _____

Section E. References

References are rarely listed on a resume, but they are a vital part of the information you need close at hand during your job search.

References should include former bosses or persons who have had a working relationship with you. A prospective employer is not interested in what your minister or your grocer thinks of you. He is only seeking information on your capabilities and work habits.

Before giving someone as a reference, ask permission. You need to ask permission each time you are job hunting. Someone willing to give you a recommendation in December 1972 may not be prepared to do so in December 1982. Of course, most persons asked to give references are happy to oblige, but courtesy demands that you ask them each time you are job hunting.

Never ask for a reference from someone who you suspect may give you a poor one. It is better not to have a reference from a place you worked than to have a damaging one.

Fill in the information requested on the forms that follow so that it will be readily available when someone asks for your references.

Reference Sheet   Although references should not go on your resume, you will want to have a ready record of them to use whenever necessary. This is what this form is for.

Reference 1

Name: _____

Company affiliation: _____

Title at company: _____

Address of company: _____

Telephone number of company or home phone: _____

Extension: _____

Reference 2

Name: _____

Company affiliation: _____

Title at company: _____

Address of company: _____

Telephone number of company or home phone: _____

Extension: _____

Reference 3

Name: _____

Company affiliation: _____

Title at company: _____

Address of company: _____

Telephone number of company or home phone: _____

Extension: _____

Reference 4

Name: _____

Company affiliation: _____

Title at company: _____

Address of company: _____

Telephone number of company or home phone: _____

Extension: _____

5 WRITING A RESUME

In chapter 4, you gathered the information you needed to write a resume and did some thinking about the purpose a resume will serve for you.

In this chapter, you will take the information you have gathered and use it to create one or more resumes to suit your individual needs. Before you do that, however, you need some knowledge about the writing style and language of resumes.

Consistency

Whatever style you decide on for your resume, you must be consistent. If you indent paragraphs three spaces in the work history or employment section, then you must indent all other paragraphs the same number of spaces. Consistency—a picky item, to be sure—is a sign that you have an organized, logical mind. And while someone may not look at your resume and think, "This person failed to indent consistently," several small errors such as this add up to a messy-looking resume.

Abbreviations

Spell out most words in a resume and use as few abbreviations as possible. About the only abbreviations that are acceptable are those for college degrees—B.A. (bachelor of arts), B.S. (bachelor of science), M.A. (master of arts), Ph.D. (doctor of philosophy). Jr. and Sr. are abbreviated, as are Mr., Mrs., and Ms. Uncommon degrees—a master's in architecture, for example—should be spelled out. Spell out the names of states, cities, streets, and avenues, and titles of persons.

Tone   One of the more difficult aspects of resume writing is mastering the tone that is most appropriate. You must avoid sounding self-important or stuffy; on the other hand, the entire point of the resume is to sell yourself, so modesty may not strike exactly the right note, either. To avoid sounding stuffy, write in plain, clear language. Rather than saying "in regard to my previous position," say "in my last position." Try to avoid such expressions as "in regard to," "in connection with," and "on or about."

The best way to avoid sounding as if you are bragging is to use specific terms and examples to back up and describe your achievements. Below are some examples of puffed language and of alternative and better ways of saying the same thing.

Too Vague
Showed excellent signs of leadership.

Performed well under stress.

Known for my energy.

Better—More Specific
Organized teams of ten persons each to study the problem.

Despite a pressing deadline, the report was ready to go in time to contribute to the merger decision.

(Omit this statement and any other statement referring to your stamina, and let everything you say specifically on the resume show that you have energy and stamina.)

Resume language is concise and goes directly to the point. You do not have a lot of space in which to express yourself, so every sentence must be well thought out.

Some resume writers add to the tone of conciseness by avoiding the use of the first person:

> Responsibilities included marketing, budgeting, and the development of a special cost-cutting unit.

While it is certainly correct to write a resume without the use of "I," there is no reason to do so, and on some occasions, the use of "I" may be necessary. It is far more important to master the skill of saying a lot in a small aount of space. The example that follows is wordy:

> In 1958, after three years of experience in the purchasing department, all of which I enjoyed immensely, I decided that the time had come to seek a greater degree of responsibility. I applied for and was granted a promotion, from assistant buyer to senior buyer, in April.

Here is a concise version of the same paragraph:

> In April 1958, promoted to full-time senior buyer.

106

Parallelism   Parallelism—making sure that the sections of the resume that are similar to one another sound alike—is important. Many persons get caught in the parallelism trap by failing to make sure that all the verb forms in a list are in the same form. Consider these two examples:

Unparallel	**Parallel**
Math major in undergraduate school	Studied math in undergraduate school
Spent senior year in France	Studied in France during senior year

Skills	*Skills*
Reading proofs	Proofing
Copy editing	Copy editing
Management of budget	Budgeting
Production skills	Production

Jargon   The word "jargon" originally referred to a meaningless kind of gibberish. Today, ironically, it refers to the inside talk or terminology of a trade or profession. Since a resume must be read by a wide range of persons—from the director of personnel who may know little or nothing of the technical aspects of the trade that he or she represents to the fifty-year-old executive who is going to hire you but feels slightly out of touch with the new terminology of his trade—jargon should be avoided. If anything, it is a rather unimpressive way of showing off.

Sounding a Positive Note   Even professional writers have to watch the tendency to write something in a negative rather than a positive way. Sometimes it shows up in a minor way, as when someone writes, "Do not fill in lines 3 and 5," rather than, "Fill in all lines except 3 and 5." Usually, though, negativism is more subtle and reflects how you feel about yourself. This is a good reason to ask a close friend to look over your resume before you put it into final form to make sure that it hits the right, upbeat tone.

Preparing the Rough Draft   Now it is time to pull the information you collected in chapter 4 and use it to prepare a rough draft of your resume. Although you presumably did the hard work of thinking about where you want to go and how to get there as you filled in the forms in chapter 4, be equally careful about filling in these forms and you will save yourself time later.

Two forms are presented: one for the historical-chronological resume and one for the skills- or achievement-oriented resume.

HISTORICAL-CHRONOLOGICAL

What heading will you use? Check one.

☐ Your name

☐ Vita

☐ Curriculum vitae

☐ Resume

☐ Resume of (your name)

Name: _____

▶ *Use only if not used in heading.*

Address: _____

City: _____

State: _____

Zip code: _____

Phone or phones: _____

Job objective: _____

_____

Employment

▶ *Begin listing with most recent job.*

Dates of employment:

From   Month _____
       Year _____

To   Month _____
       Year _____

Job title: _____

Name of company: _____

Address of company: _____

▶ *The above is not optional material.*

Description of duties and responsibilities: _____

_____

_____

_____

▶ *Try to pare down and write this in resume-style language. Remember to note individual projects as well as daily responsibilities. Repeat this information on separate sheets of paper until you have described all relevant jobs. Attach sheets to this form.*

Education

From   Month _____
        Year _____

To   Month _____
        Year _____

School: _____

Year graduated: _____

Degree: _____

Major areas of study: _____

▶ *Repeat this information, moving from school you must recently attended back to high school, and write it on separate sheets of paper. Attach to this form.*

Personal

Birth date: _____

Marital status: _____

Willingness to travel: _____

Willingness to relocate: _____

▶ *Circle either of the two items above if you plan to use.*

Optional Categories

▶ *Fill these in only if they apply to you or your career area.*

Languages (name and level of fluency): _____
_____

Publications (briefly describe your writing experiences):
_____
_____
_____

▶ *On a separate sheet, list correct bibliographical information, books first and articles second.*

Military Service

Branch: _____

Dates served: _____

Rank of discharge: _____

Any special training or skills: _____

_____

_____

Volunteer Work

Name of group: _____

Position or title: _____

Number of years involved: From _____ to _____

Describe, as much as possible in terms that relate to business, your
responsibilities and achievements in the group: _____

_____

_____

_____

_____

▶ *Repeat this information on separate sheets of paper until you have noted all
relevant volunteer work. Remember to list unofficial work, i.e., running
garage sales, benefits, etc. Attach to this form.*

Skills List

If you have a set of specific skills (office or publishing production
skills, for example), list them below. Then rewrite the list separately,
making sure that all the items are parallel.

1. _____

2. _____

3. _____

4. _____

5. _____

6. _____

▶ *Do not use numbers in the final skills list.*

SKILLS- OR ACHIEVEMENT-ORIENTED

What heading will you use? Check one.

☐ Your name

☐ Vita

☐ Curriculum vitae

☐ Resume

☐ Resume of (your name)

Name: _____

▶ *Use only if not used in heading.*

Address: _____

City: _____

State: _____

Zip code: _____

Phone or phones: _____

Job objective: _____

_____

Summary or capsule of your experience: _____

_____

_____

_____

▶ *Divide the capsule into areas of involvement or expertise. Write in paragraph form, using the first person. This section should be written almost in letter form. Use paragraphs if necessary.*

Employment History

▶ *Begin with most recently held job.*

From   Month _____
        Year _____

To   Month _____
        Year _____

111

Job title: _____

Name of company: _____

▶ *Repeat this information on separate sheets of paper until you have described all relevant jobs. Attach sheets to this form.*

Personal

Birth date: _____

Marital status: _____

Willingness to travel

Willingness to relocate

▶ *Circle either of the two items above if you plan to use.*

Education

Degree: _____

School: _____

Year graduated: _____

Major areas of study: _____

▶ *Repeat this information, moving from the school you most recently attended back to high school, or your B.A. if you have advanced degrees, and write it on separate sheets of paper. Attach to this form.*

▶ *For optional categories, turn to HISTORICAL-CHRONOLOGICAL resume form and fill in information in the categories you require.*

Once you have completed whichever of these forms applies to you, the task of transferring this information to rough, type- or hand-written form should be relatively easy. In fact, you should have to do only minor editing of what you have written on the forms.

You now have your resume in hand. All you have to do is have it typed in final form and reproduced.

CHECKLIST

Before having your resume typed in final form, check it against this list to make sure that you have included all the important items of information.

☐ Heading (Resume, your name, job title)

☐ Name

☐ Address and apartment number

☐ City or town

☐ State

☐ Zip code

☐ Telephone numbers

☐ Work history

    ☐ Correct dates of employment

    ☐ Names of companies

    ☐ Titles you held

☐ Education

    ☐ Names of schools

    ☐ Dates of graduation or years attended

    ☐ Degrees awarded

☐ Personal information

    ☐ Birth date (not age)

    ☐ Marital status

    ☐ Willingness to relocate

    ☐ Willingness to travel

    ☐ Any other information you plan to include

☐ Military service

    ☐ Dates served

    ☐ Rank on discharge

    ☐ Special training

    ☐ Special duties

☐ Languages

☐ Publications

☐ Professional memberships

☐ Statement about references, samples, or portfolio

6

THE COVER LETTER

A personnel consultant hired to help a middle-sized manufac-turing company find a new president ran an ad in *The Wall Street Journal* asking for applications for the position. He received approximately 175 replies. Of these, about half were obviously from persons who were answering any ad that came along. Their resumes were general in tone, and their cover letters might have been sent to any U.S. manufacturing company.

Only six applicants stood out. They did so because their resumes were accompanied by outstanding cover letters in which each person outlined why he believed he was the person the company was seeking. The letters, the consultant reported, made him turn to the resumes attached to them. The cover letters, however, were what first caught his eye, introduced him to the applicants, and heightened the importance of the resumes that accompanied them.

Cover letters are at least as important as the resume you write, and every resume should be sent with a cover letter.

A cover letter has two formal purposes: it introduces you or announces your resume, and it gets you an interview. While the resume sells you and describes what you have done professionally, only the cover letter actually asks for an interview. And any good salesperson knows that if you don't make the move to close the sale, you are likely to lose it. While getting an interview is hardly the final step in getting a job, failing to ask for an interview in a cover letter may well be the *only* reason you do not get one.

The Tone of the Cover Letter

The cover letter must grab the reader and make him or her want to read your resume. This is why a cover letter should highlight the most important items in your resume or the achievements that you think will most impress the reader.

115

A cover letter should always be as personal as you can make it. If possible, get the name and title of the person to whom you are writing. One simple way to do this is to call the company and ask for the name of the vice president of operations or the comptroller or whoever will have ultimate responsibility for hiring you. Source-books like those Dun & Bradstreet publishes are also helpful in locating names and addresses.

Even if you have slanted your resume to a particular company, it must still follow the prescribed format and should include only certain items of information. A cover letter, on the other hand, can —and should—slip in that achievement of which you are extraordinarily proud or emphasize how you have saved the company money or how you have reorganized departments you have been responsible for.

A cover letter should tell the recipient exactly what he or she wants to hear. If a company is looking for a salesperson who has increased sales in other firms, and you feel that your major strength lies in introducing new sales lines, you should explain how you increased sales for your firm. The cover letter is probably not the place to bring up other achievements, once you know what the recipient of the letter is looking for. Don't dilute your sales strength.

How a Cover Letter Should Look

Try to have your own stationery printed for use in cover letters. It should be 8½ by 11 inches. White is always a safe color, although buff, light brown, manila and pale gray are also acceptable. Using a color for your stationery can pose a problem if your resume is printed on white, as most resumes are. Resumes on colored paper are not as acceptable as colored stationery, and the white paper of your resume beside your stationery may not look too good. When purchasing stationery, give thought to how it will coordinate with your resume.

Stationery should be a high-quality bond, with your vital mailing statistics printed or engraved on it. Above all, keep it simple, avoiding such typographical devices as lines or rules, cute drawings, and small symbols. Printed information should include your name, address, city, state, town and zip, as well as a telephone number. This may be centered or set flush left or right, whatever pleases your eye. Your stationer can advise you about format. Stick to a plain typeface. Order matching envelopes, printed with the same information minus your phone number.

Costs of stationery vary widely, as does quality, so if money is a consideration, shop around until you find someone who meets your price range and your standards for quality.

Keeping a Record of Cover Letters

As you mail cover letters and resumes to prospective employers, keep a written record of the transaction as well as carbon copies of the letters. After an appropriate amount of time, call for an appointment.

A written record of your correspondence might look like this:

Company	Date sent	Interview	Thank-you note sent	Follow-up comments
ABC	8/5/81	8/20/81	8/21/81	No job now; opening expected mid-Sept.
LMP	8/5/81	None	8/17/81	Check back late Sept.
XYZ	8/5/81	8/23/81	8/23/81	They will call

Format of the Cover Letter

The cover letter and the thank-you note should be written in the standard format of a business letter. The parts of the business letter are shown on page 118.

Between the air of informality that pervades business today and the voices of feminism, knowing how to address someone can be a major problem. Ideally, of course, you would have the name and title of the person to whom you are writing and could therefore avoid entirely the somewhat awkward use of "Dear Sir or Ma'am." If this is not possible, you may stick to the more old-fashioned "Sir" or you may write "Dear Sir or Ma'am."

Which of the current titles to use for a woman—Ms., Miss, or Mrs.—is a personal decision unless you have some way of determining what the receiver would like to read. Ms. has become acceptable in most urban areas of the country; it is slightly less so in smaller communities and rural areas.

If you have not met the person to whom you are writing, you are probably taking too great a risk in using a first name in the greeting. Someone you know and call by his or her first name would be addressed that way in the greeting, although you should spell the name in full in the inside address.

The heading will probably be centered if you have had stationery printed; otherwise, type it flush right. On printed stationery, you can type the date under your printed heading if it looks satisfactory, or you can type it several lines below and flush right.

The inside address must be as complete as possible. Do not abbreviate anything on the inside heading, except what is shown in the example. If a line is too long to look right going across the page, type it in two lines and indent the second line, as shown in the example:

HEADING

Kevin Greene
587 Tremont Street
Indianapolis, Indiana 49744
September 12, 19_

INSIDE
ADDRESS
Mr. William Jamison
Mutual Life Insurance Company
690 Meridian Lane
Indianapolis, Indiana 49744

GREETING Dear Mr. Jamison:

BODY OF
LETTER
Thank you very much for meeting with me last Thursday. I was very impressed to learn about your training program, as I had been told I would be by Bob Jones. I hope you will keep me in mind for any future openings.

CLOSE Sincerely,

SIGNATURE *Kevin Greene*

TYPED NAME Kevin Greene

Mr. Jack Roth, Jr.
Assistant to the Vice President
  of Operations
First Federal Savings & Loan
1900 Main Street
Columbus, Idaho 00000

Leave fairly wide margins and a generous amount of space at the top and bottom of the page. Since neither a cover letter nor a thank-you note should run longer than one page, try to center the letter so that it looks nice on the page. A business letter must be typed. Handwritten letters are never acceptable, nor are letters that do not pretty much follow the format just described.

Close the letter with something simple; "Sincerely" or "Cordially" will do. You should leave three or four spaces in which to sign your name, and then type your name below that. Always type your full name, even if you plan to sign only your first name. Do not type a title under your name. Even if you are employed at the time, you are not writing this letter in behalf of the company, so there is no reason to use your title.

The same advice, by the way, applies to using a company's stationery for your job-hunting activities. It not only looks bad, but could cause a future employer to wonder what you might pilfer from him.

What to Say in a Cover Letter

Keep a cover letter brief; it should rarely run more than one page. Only if the person to whom the letter is sent is well-known to you should you go into lengthy detail about how you could handle the job or save his or her company money. Unsolicited advice—and sometimes even solicited advice—is more often than not unwelcome in business.

In fact, only if you have been invited very seriously to comment about a company should you launch into a discourse on how to improve the company. Too many ill-advised persons use this attention-getting device in their cover letters only to discover too late that it gets the wrong kind of attention.

A cover letter to someone you do not know—when you are answering a blind ad, for instance—should highlight one or two of your achievements. Most cover letters consist of four paragraphs, in which you do the following—

1. State that you would like to work for the company, making sure to mention the company by name.
2. Tell why you want to work for the company.
3. Describe the qualifications you would bring to them.
4. Request an interview with them.

In paragraph 2, you aim to catch the reader's interest. You can say you have been watching his product for a while and are impressed

119

with how it is marketed, or that you want to learn a certain skill and feel that this company would be the best place to do so, or that you want to develop a specialty further and feel that XYZ, Inc., is the place to do so. Be frank and slightly forward, but do not gush.

In paragraph 3, give only two or three reasons that you are qualified to work for the company. If at all possible, make sure they are qualifications the company is seeking. Save the other reasons and lengthy explanations for your resume.

In paragraph 4, say that you are free for an interview. Persons looking for a first job or others with little experience can get away with suggesting an appropriate interview time: "I do not have classes on Fridays and wonder if I might arrange to talk with you then," or "I shall be in New York next Wednesday and Thursday, and hope we might set up an appointment on one of those days." Once you have held a few jobs and are going for a higher-level job, this ploy no longer is acceptable, and more subtlety is called for. You should definitely suggest an interview, but the time and place are best left to the person who will be seeing you.

The exception to this is when you are job hunting in one community and you live in another; then you can suggest certain days when you will be available for interviewing.

After a week and a half to ten days, plan to follow up a cover letter and a resume with a phone call, in which you attempt to firm up the appointment time and place.

Answering Blind Ads

Responding to a blind ad, one in which no company identification is offered, is a disheartening experience at best. It is particularly difficult on lower-level jobs advertised in daily newspapers; these ads often generate hundreds of responses, and more often than not, you will never get any answer to your resume and letter. Blind ads in business newspapers such as *The Wall Street Journal* or in professional journals are a different matter. Often the company is not identified because it feels the need to be confidential—and often you can figure out what the company is or at least make some assumptions about it from what the ad says.

The most awkward aspect of answering a blind ad is the greeting. Impersonal as it may seem, you have little choice but to direct the letter to the box number or whatever other address is given. The heading should probably read: "Dear Sir" or "Dear Sir or Ma'am."

Keep a careful record of any ads you respond to, plus a copy of the cover letter that accompanies your resume, because this is the only information you will have if you do receive a reply.

What you say in a cover letter written in response to a blind ad depends upon what information you are given in the ad. If you are given a lot of information about the job requirements, job experience, and type of work involved, you can respond by pointing out how your experience and training meshes with what the company seems to be seeking. On page 121 is a sample blind ad and a cover-letter response.

**ADMINISTRATIVE ASS'T
ADVERTISING**

Mad. Ave. advertising agency seeks indiv.
to assist with research projects, also help
acc't executive with progress reports and
client liaison.

January 31, 19__
2701 Meadow Lane
Brooklyn, New York 10012

Box 210
New York Times
New York, New York 10036

Dear Sir or Ma'am:

This letter is in response to your advertisement in the Monday, January 31,
New York Times.

I believe that I may have the qualifications you are seeking. I have
worked in advertising for six years, beginning as a secretary and working
my way up to my current position as administrative assistant with a major
Madison Avenue agency. My responsibilities include preparing dossiers on
clients, product research, typing and light editing of progress reports,
and client contact, primarily by telephone. Although I am happy with my
current position, I am seeking a position that will afford me greater
opportunity for client-liaison work. Your position would seem to offer
that responsibility.

If you feel that I have the experience and skills you require, I would
very much like to meet with you personally to discuss the job. I am
enclosing a copy of my resume, which further details my work experience.
I look forward to meeting with you.

Sincerely,

Jeanne Howell

Jeanne Howell

*Cover letter in response to sample
blind ad*

If the blind ad offers very little information, then a fairly impersonal cover letter is probably the best you can do. Consider writing something like the letter on this page.

December 7, 19__
20 East Ninety-fourth Street
New York, New York 10022

Box 201
St. Louis Courier-Journal
St. Louis, Missouri 38470

Dear Sir or Ma'am:

This letter is in response to your ad of Sunday, December 3, 1978, in the St. Louis Courier-Journal. I feel that I may have many of the qualifications you are seeking, and am enclosing a copy of my resume, which describes my work experience and training in detail.

I would welcome the opportunity to meet with you personally to discuss your requirements for filling this position.

Sincerely,

Tania Oblesky

Tania Oblesky

Cover letter in response to blind ad

Content of the Cover Letter—New Graduates   If you have little or no real work experience, a cover letter will be brief, like the one on this page.

Jack Danielson, Jr.
5970 King Drive South
Chicago, Illinois 60628
September 1, 19—

Mr. Sidney Graham
Director of Personnel
CRT Manufacturing, Inc.
1900 Corporate Lane
Baltimore, Maryland 21200

Dear Mr. Graham:

I am writing to inquire about the possibility of work in CRT's personnel management training program.

My special interest in your program derives from the fact that I have spent a major part of this year working on a master's thesis about new personnel techniques developed at CRT.

I am currently completing my M.B.A. at the University of Chicago, with a specialty in personnel.

I shall be in Baltimore on September 20 and 21, and wonder if we might meet to discuss this further at that time. I shall call your office next week to see about the possibility of confirming an appointment.

Sincerely,

Jack Danielson, Jr.
Jack Danielson, Jr.

Cover letter for someone with little work experience

Content of the Cover Letter—Experienced Workers

Someone with experience would, of course, write more. Persons applying for a middle-management position might write a cover letter resembling those that begin on this page.

Jeanette Beane
450 Melrose Lane
Palo Alto, California 94303

December 15, 19___

Ms. Evelun Beckmann
Director of Cosmetics Development
Rosemont Cosmetics, Inc.
30000 Roundhill Drive
Palo Alto, California 94305

Dear Ms. Beckmann:

This letter is to inquire about the possibility of obtaining work in cosmetics development at Rosemont Cosmetics.

I presently work for a competitive firm, where I am involved in the development of skin-care creams. I am aware of Rosemont's reputation for quality in the skin-care line, and because I am most interested in pursuing this line, I am especially eager to discuss the possibility of a senior research position at Rosemont.

I have ten years of experience in cosmetology and a doctorate from the Institute of Cosmetology in biochemistry. I was largely responsible for the development of my present employer's line of skin-care products, and I have some interesting ideas for new products.

Would it be possible for us to meet to discuss this further? I shall call your office early next week to inquire about an appointment.

Sincerely,

Jeanette Beane

Jeanette Beane

Cover letter for experienced worker

Derek Mann
33 Ivy Lane
Nashville, Tennessee 37212
April 14, 19___

Talia Wedgwood
3 Potters Row
Nashville, Tennessee 37212

Dear Ms. Wedgwood:

This letter is to inquire about the possibility of joining the Potters Studio.

I am familiar with your reputation in black-on-black pottery and wish to study with you to learn more about it.

I have studied pottery under George Sienne at the Mt. Tamalpais Workshop for three years, and I currently exhibit in his shop and at the Pottery Store in Michigan.

Would it be possible for us to meet to discuss this further? My phone number is 860-1099. I shall eagerly await your answer. I shall also be happy to bring samples of my work to show you.

Sincerely,

Derek Mann
Derek Mann

Cover letter for experienced worker

George Jamison
875 North Michigan Avenue
Apartment 3007
Chicago, Illinois 60611
October 3, 19__

Mr. Donald Neely
Senior Editor
Olympia Press
50 West Forty-ninth Street
New York, New York 10020

Dear Mr. Neely:

This letter is to inquire about the possibility of an opening in the
editorial department of Olympia Press.

Your reputation for publishing quality anthropology books is known throughout publishing and in anthropology, and I have always been hopeful that one
day I might be able to combine my education in anthropology and my experience
in publishing. Olympia Press seems to offer the best opportunity for doing
that.

I have five years' experience in trade-book editing. I also have a Ph.D.
in anthropology and have done field work in Cuba on the status of women in
the sugar-cane fields, which resulted in the publication of a book by
Julian Press. I am bilingual, Spanish and English, which I mention because
I am familiar with your many fine Spanish-language books.

I would be delighted to meet with you at your convenience to discuss this
further. My phone number is 548-0900. I look forward to hearing from you.

Cordially,

George Jamison

George Jamison

Cover letter for experienced worker

Maria Sayers
40 River Drive
Princeton, New Jersey 08540
May 20, 19__

Sarton, Jones, and Sarton, Counselors
1300 Main Street
Princeton, New Jersey 18540

Dear Mr. Jones:

I am writing to inquire about the possibility of working for Sarton, Jones,
and Sarton.

I have long admired your work in tax law, and have always hoped that one
day it might be possible for me to be in a position to learn from this firm.

After earning my master's of law from New York University, I applied with
Sarton, Jones, and Sarton, only to learn that you never take on new
graduates. In the intervening six years, I have been working in the tax
department of Siliback and Siliback, and have been involved in several
major tax and antitrust cases.

Would it be possible for us to meet to discuss this further? I can be
reached by phone at 226-0400. I shall eagerly await your reply.

Sincerely,

Maria Sayers

Maria Sayers

Cover letter for experienced worker

John Boll
1400 Seneca Drive
Alexandria, Virginia 22305
March 17, 19__

Thomas McKay
Director of Operations
Computron DataProducts, Inc.
St. Louis, Missouri 63119

Dear Mr. McKay:

I am writing to inquire about any possible openings that Computron
DataProducts may have in operations.

I am especially interested in coming to work for you because for the past
two and one-half years, I have been working with your Comput 2600 system,
and I am most impressed with it. I have a strong interest in the
development of computer lines and know your reputation for quality.

I hold a B.S. in computer science and have ten years of experience in the
field. I have worked in both sales and technology. In my present
capacity as director of computer operations, I have been responsible for
introducing and setting up the Comput 2600 system.

Would it be possible to arrange a meeting so that we might further discuss
the possibility of my coming to work for you? My phone number is 282-0333.

Sincerely,

John Boll

John Boll

Cover letter for experienced worker

Cover letters require time and thought. While a cover letter will rarely take as much time to prepare as a resume will, it can hardly be dashed off. Do not become frustrated if you find yourself spending the better part of a morning on a single letter. It is important enough to be worth the time.

FINISHING TOUCHES

At last your resume is typed and ready to go. You have done as much work on it as you possibly can, and you feel that you have given it your best effort. It is ready to be reproduced and mailed out to prospective employers.

Now there are just a few more things to think about. First, because your resume may be the only impression you make, it must be checked and double-checked for accuracy of facts, correct spelling, and proper grammar. There are two steps you can take to ensure that your resume is as well done in this department as possible. First, put it away for a few days and forget about it. Then take it out and read it carefully again. Often you will spot something that does not sound exactly right, or notice a misspelled word or some other detail that is not exactly correct. Second, ask a friend or someone you know is good at grammar and spelling to look it over for any errors you may have missed. It does take extra effort to correct a resume at this stage—you're probably ready to be done with it—but make the effort. For all your care, someone will probably read your resume in five minutes, if that long, and spot a glaring error that will almost surely cause it to be tossed into the wastebasket. It definitely pays to have another pair of eyes take a look at your resume. One woman who was applying for the position of bank vice-president let her nine-year-old daughter take a look at the last draft of her resume and was both delighted and dismayed when the child spotted a grammatical error.

MAKING COPIES OF YOUR RESUME

Since resumes get passed out in quantity, you will need a way to make copies of your resume. You do not have to send individually typed copies, although you may occasionally want to take such pains with a resume that you are slanting very specifically toward a job you know you want.

There are two ways to duplicate your resume: by copy machine (such as Xerox) and by offset printing. Both procedures are usually handled by the same person. Look in the Yellow Pages under "instant printers," as the people who do this work are called. If you don't see the term "instant printer," there are other advertising words that indicate the type of printer you need. They are "rush work," "same day service," "photo copy," and "fast offset printing." These may not be the exact words in the ads, but anything to this effect indicates a small printer who will be willing to handle the kind of job you have in mind. If in doubt, call and ask whether he can duplicate your resume for you.

Instant printers vary greatly in quality, so you should ask to see some samples of work before you let a printer have your job. These printers can also help you print business cards and stationery, if you need it. They can also sell you plain paper stock to match the paper they print your resume on.

Instant printers vary greatly in price, so you should shop around before you make a final decision. They offer a price break if you print in quantity—for some printers, this means more than 100 copies and for others, more than 500 copies. Ask the printer's advice before you choose a printing method. If you want only ten or twelve copies, you probably want your resume run through a duplicating machine; if you want sixty copies, it still might be cheaper to have one hundred or whatever the minimum is printed by the offset or photo copy method. Offset printing always gives better quality than a duplicating machine does.

One good way to find a suitable instant printer is to ask friends for recommendations.

When you bring your resumes home from the printer, store them in a place where they will stay clean and unmessed. Each resume you send must look crisp, clean, and new.

MAILING YOUR RESUME

Fold a couple of resumes with sample sheets of stationery to see what kind of fold and what kind of envelope you will need. Never mail a resume in an envelope so small that a vertical fold is required. Sometimes a two- or three-page resume will not fit easily into a regular-size envelope. In that case, use a 6-by-9 or 9-by-12 envelope. That way, you can fold the resume in half once, or you can mail it perfectly flat. Larger-size envelopes have another advantage: they stand out in the morning mail.

Always find out exactly what postage your resume and cover letter require. Don't assume they can be mailed at the going rate for a first-class letter, particularly if you are using a large envelope. Making a company you would like to work for pay extra postage to find out what you are all about will never help you get the job.

Mass Mailings
If you are going to do a mass mailing of your resume and cover letters, break the task into separate steps. This is monotonous work, so it helps to enlist the neighborhood kids' assistance, if at all possible.

First, staple the sheets of your resume together if necessary. Then fold. Then stuff envelopes. Then lick the postage. Mindless as the work is, it doesn't take much time, and mass mailings can pay off. You can expect a 1 or 2 percent response rate on one, which should help you decide whether a mass mailing is worth it for your resume.

As your supply of resumes runs low, be sure to keep a couple of copies for your records.

After Mailing Your Resume
About a week and a half to two weeks after mailing your resume, you can touch base with the person you sent it to. Call and request an appointment for an interview, mentioning in the phone conversation that you sent your resume on such-and-such a day. Sometimes someone is interested in you, but assumes that you will get in touch, so always follow up by phone on a mailed resume, if possible.

Whether or not you get an interview, a thank-you note is a nice touch.

THANK-YOU NOTES—MAKING CONTACTS

A thank-you note may seem a bit extravagant, especially if you have not managed to get your foot in the door for an interview, but part of getting a job is having contacts with prospective employers— and one way of building those contacts is to remind people just as often as possible that you exist. Every time your name crosses someone's desk, the chances increase that it will ring a bell the next time.

You may stand out in someone's memory because you were the applicant who wrote a thank-you note. And when another job opening comes along—one that is especially suited to your skills and talents—someone may just remember you a little better than the other applicants because of the one small, extra contact with you.

A sample of a thank-you note follows.

Ann Rockwell
3778 Newport Road
Albuquerque, New Mexico 87100
Phone: 833-3010
February 5, 19__

Ms. Phyllis Knight
Vice President, Personnel
Vue Limited
800 Boswell Street
Venice, Ohio 45174

Dear Ms. Knight:

I enjoyed talking with you Monday about the prospect of coming
to work at Vue. I especially appreciated hearing of Vue's
track record with women, which is outstanding. When Vue has
an opening, I hope you will have me in mind. I feel that my
qualifications and work experience would fit in well at Vue.

Again, thank you for your time.

Sincerely,

Ann Rockwell

Ann Rockwell

REVISING YOUR RESUME

If you have followed the steps listed in this book and have saved this book as your permanent resume record, revising a resume should be a relatively simple and painless task.

Resumes become outdated when some piece of personal information changes (a good reason to include as little as possible), when you lose a job, or when you decide to look for a new job.

• *To update your resume:* Read it carefully, circling in red ink any items that are no longer accurate. On separate sheets of paper, write in substitute information blocks for the ones that need to be changed.

• If some item needs to be dropped entirely, cross it out.

• Some persons date resumes. If you have done this, remember to change the date.

• Read over your changes to make sure they follow the style and format of your old resume. Retype your resume, adding new information as needed.

88

TITLE #	TITLE	PRICE
	Plus Additional $1.00 Per Book for Postage	
	Grand Total	$

MONARCH PRESS, Mail Service Department, BT, 1230 Avenue of the Americas, New York, New York 10020

I enclose $_____ to cover retail price plus mailing and handling.
NY residents please add applicable sales tax.

Name_____
(PLEASE PRINT)

Address_____

City_____ State_____ Zip Code_____

Please send check or money order. We cannot be responsible for cash.